Life Injections III

Additional Connections of Scripture to the Human Experience

Richard E. Zajac

PublishAmerica
Baltimore

First printing

ISBN: 1-4241-7488-0
PUBLISHED BY PUBLISHAMERICA, LLLP
www.publishamerica.com
Baltimore

Printed in the United States of America

In loving memory of Father William G. Stanton:

my mentor
my role model
my friend

Table of Contents

Introduction 7
A Wonderful Life 9
The Awful Kindnesses of Others 17
Offenses of the Spirit 23
What's a Perfectionist to Do? 29
Is Your Halo on Too Tight? 36
A Tonic of Huge and Big Things 42
Three-O'clock-in-the-Morning Courage 49
Almost 55
Yes 61
A Troubling Friendship 67
Saying Thank You 73
The Devil's Favorite Tool 79
Five Minutes Longer 85
Playing It Safe 91
Disconnection 97
Closing the Gate 103
The Voice of God 109
We're in This Together 115
Blacksmith's Creed 119
A Name and a Face 125
Secrets 130
Flexibility 136
Elephants & Mice 141
Being Radiant 146
Giving Attention 152
Motors Always Running 158
Losing Jesus 164
Lord, Teach Us to Pray 170
Endnotes 177

Introduction

In the introductions to my two previous books, I reflected on my inspiration for good preaching and outlined the painstaking process I follow when the challenge to compose a new sermon sits before me. In this latest installment of Sunday reflections, I thought I might share some of my frustrations and thoughts concerning the enterprise known as preaching.

As you can tell from the length of the following sermons, I violate the five- to seven-minute rule most Catholic preachers tend to follow. As a result, my presence at certain pulpits is not very welcomed. It's sad as to how some of our most popular Catholic Churches are those where speed and brevity are of the essence, where the congregant can make it out the building in less than 25 minutes. Perhaps they have been driven there by unprepared preachers who ramble on and on and then find it difficult to "land the plane," or perhaps they just prefer a "McDonald's" approach to worship. I happen to believe that God deserves better and God's Word commands more than just a passing glance. But maybe it's just me.

I put a tremendous amount of value on good preaching and although I acknowledge and applaud those who do it well in five to seven minutes, I find myself wanting to go a bit further (I hover around the fifteen-minute mark); I find myself wishing to provide the extra point or the extra nuance that might just be what some congregant needs to hear to change his or her life. Too many points to ponder? Perhaps! Too small a focus on the Scriptures? I suppose so! Too much psychology, not enough theology? I'll accept that criticism! Too many stories? You might say that! But I don't believe there's any doubt that the finished product is reflective of rigorous hours of hard work and effort and few, if any, would find it a bore. The sermons may be too long for some but hopefully not long enough for those truly searching for a meaningful sermon, truly hoping to find the relevance of God's word when it comes to the living of their life.

The driving force behind my preaching can be found in a line attributed to St. Ireneaus: "the glory of God is a man or woman fully alive!" The following 28 sermons are geared towards precisely that, geared towards the reader realizing their full potential, geared towards their realizing and acting on the obstacles and the mindsets and the behavior thwarting their ability to live life to the full. On these following pages, you'll also find reflections on the whereabouts of God's voice, the ways and means of prayer as well as to why God's friends might happen to number so very few. I hope you'll enjoy these humbled attempts to once again connect Scripture to the human experience.

A Wonderful Life

Scripture Lesson: Matthew 25: 31-46
"...Whenever you did it for one of my least brothers and sisters, you did it for me..."

The following is my eulogy for my friend and mentor Bill Stanton, in whose memory this book is dedicated.

This very day draws a close to the Christmas season and so I'm given the liberty of referencing a yuletide illustration, in particular, the Frank Capra's movie classic: *It's a Wonderful Life*. We all know the story. George Bailey, played by James Stewart, lives in the fictional town of Bedford Falls N.Y. where he marries a beautiful girl, starts a family, and finds success as the owner of a Buildings and Loan Association. Hard times strike the banking industry and when George's Uncle Billy loses a bank deposit of $8,000, it appears the Building and Loan Association would have to close and with it would come bankruptcy, scandal and prison time for George Bailey. Totally distraught, Bailey considers taking his own life figuring the insurance money would cover that $8,000 loss.

As he stands on a bridge intending to jump, his guardian angel Clarence Oddbody appears hoping to convince him not to do it. George complains to Oddbody that the world would be better off without him, that the world would be better off if he had never been born. Clarence decides to show him that it wasn't true. As George heads back to town, he gets to see how bereft Bedford Falls would be and how impoverished many a life would be had he, in fact, never been born. The movie ends with George Bailey in the parlor of his house surrounded by his family and all his many friends. They had anteed up the money to save the bank and it was in testimony to all the wonderful things he did on their behalf. George Bailey comes to realize that the world wouldn't have been better off without him. He'd come to realize that he had in fact lived a wonderful life.

William George Stanton lived a wonderful life and the fact is that many a place would be bereft, many a life would be impoverished, had he never been born. Take St. Bridget's Parish in Newfane, New York. Its parishioners would never have realized the fruits of empowerment, they would never have come to the understanding that they and not the pastor were the church, that the responsibility for the running of the parish rested in their hands.

One of Bill's favorite stories involved a meeting of the personnel board. He and the other members of the board were interviewing several candidates interested in the pastorate of a particular parish. The process concludes with a vote taken by the board as to whom would be the best man for the job. The results are sent up to the Bishop who makes the ultimate appointment. Well, in the course of an interview of a particular priest, Bill asked him what his thoughts were as to a parish council, what his thoughts were about empowering people. The priest barked back: "You mean like Newfane!" Bill, who was pastor at St. Ambrose at the time, said: "Yes, I guess you'd say like in Newfane." "You left the place a mess!" said the priest, "The people there think that they own the place!" The priest in question called Bill the following day to apologize. Bill accepted the apology but then informed him that "he voted yesterday." The parish and the people of St. Bridget's Church in Newfane would be greatly impoverished had Bill Stanton not been born.

If Bill Stanton had never been born, many a life of an alumnus of Bishop Turner High School would have been greatly impoverished. As many of you know, Bill spent many years at Turner as a teacher as well as the vice principal and that latter role carried with it the responsibility of administering discipline. I can think of one kid in particular who probably possesses the best attendance record at his present place of employment thanks to Bill's creative disciplinary tactics. The kid I'm referring to had the habit of missing school on Mondays and one Monday Bill had a little extra time on his hands. He goes to the kid's house and knocks on the door. His grandmother answers and she's glad to see him because her grandson had gone back to bed once his mother left for work and he wouldn't respond to her pleas for him to go to school. Bill asked her where his bedroom happened to be and went right to it. Upon entering the room, Bill pulled the kid out of bed and threw him onto the floor. (A more memorable wake up call I'm sure he'd never had.) Bill says to him, "Get dressed, you're going to school!" When he got the kid to school, he parked his car in the farthest extremity of the parking lot so he could parade him past several classroom windows, driving home the point to anyone who saw them that they'd better perish the thought of ever skipping school.

Along with such "over the top" disciplinary tactics were the ones Bill gleaned from the Marquis de Sade. Students deft at spitballs might be found on all fours pushing a spitball down a long corridor with their nose, and misbehaving in general often resulted in the guilty party kneeling in a squat position reading poetry for a half an hour at a time.

One of Bill's favorite tactics was to have the wayward child come to his office. While the kid would be waiting to see him, Bill would be loudly barking orders to his secretary (with tongue firmly in cheek, of course) asking that she put together transfer papers for Kensington High School. She was also to look up the boy's father's work number so the father might be informed of the transfer. The kid, hearing all of this, would be beside himself in fear and terror. When he'd finally get called into Bill's office, he was like putty in Bill's hands. He'd be begging for mercy, promising never to give misbehaving a second thought.

There are many a Bishop Turner High School alumnus in the community who have Bill to thank for keeping them on the straight and the narrow, who have Bill to thank for giving them guidance and direction and inspiration, who have greatly benefited from the wisdom and the example and the care which Bill provided them. Many a life of a Turner High alumnus would be greatly impoverished had Bill Stanton never been born.

And so it can be said for many a life of a Sister of Mercy. I've lost track of who is presently on the Mercy leadership team, but I'm willing to bet that each one of them was taught at one time or another by Bill Stanton. In Bill's early years as a priest, he was a regular instructor of the novices of the Mercy order. His teaching style, his charisma endeared him to many and especially so was the fact that he was their window to the outside world. Back in the days of old, novices couldn't read newspapers, listen to the radio or watch television. So whenever the novice mistress left the room, Bill would stray from his lecture and begin commentating on the news stories of the day. He'd relay to the novices the goings on of the Vatican Council, the results of local elections, and the teams participating in the World Series, as well as tantalizing bits and pieces of neighborhood gossip.

And besides being their teacher, Bill was a confidante and a confessor to many a Mercy and left an indelible mark on many of their hearts. What most won him their admiration and appreciation was his advocacy of the role of women in the church. Bill trumpeted many a feminist cause and didn't let a Vatican ban stop him from talking about women's ordination. Many a life of a Sister of Mercy would be greatly impoverished had Bill Stanton never been born.

And so would the Diocese of Buffalo be greatly impoverished as well. I don't know how many of you are familiar with Bill's younger days as a priest but back then he helped found and then lead a group known as the Priest's Association. The Association was comprised of priests not at all pleased with the way some of their brothers had been treated by the chancery office nor were they at all pleased about some of the positions the Diocese had taken on some of the more important issues of the day. The Association made a lot of noise and rattled more than a few cages and their doing so gave much strength and comfort to many a disgruntled priest as well as many a disgruntled Catholic. As you might well imagine, the Association was not a favorite of Bishop James McNulty as the two fought many a battle. Bill got labeled as "a crafty politician" by Bishop McNulty and, interestingly enough, also labeled as "one of his finest" by the very same Bishop shortly before he would die.

In the friendlier days of Bishop Head, Bill served several terms on the Priest's Council and was elected as its president for a good portion of his term. Thanks to his leadership many a welcomed change was made to better this Diocese. Yes, the Diocese of Buffalo would be greatly impoverished had Bill Stanton not been born.

So, too, would be the presbyterate of this Diocese. I don't need to tell you that Bill was a great mimic. He could mouth the stereotypical accent of each and every nationality and wasn't adverse to using that talent to fool and trap unsuspecting priests. I can remember his calling a mutual friend of ours who had just been named pastor of an Irish parish and with his patented Irish brogue pretend to be a parishioner decrying the German heritage of the new pastor. The guy fell for it hook, line, and sinker.

There were also the famous priests' parties where a few glasses of Dewar's and soda would prime Bill to do his famous Bishop Leo Smith imitation, Smith being the Diocesan Chancellor at the time. It wouldn't be long thereafter when his buddies would get him to call one of the priests and as "Bishop Leo Smith" inform him of a change of assignment usually to a parish where the priest would have dreaded to go. Some went so far as to pack their bags only to be informed at the eleventh hour that the great mimic Stanton had scored again.

And besides his being a great mimic, Bill was also a masterful storyteller and would regale us for hours with stories which, though we had heard them ten times over, never lost their humor. He'd love to tell of the antics of Monsignor Leo Toomey, the legendary pastor St. Teresa's Parish. A favorite was the time someone swore at Msgr. Toomey while he was directing traffic in front of the church. He caught the license number of the car and later asked Bill's dad, who was a police officer at the time, to trace it to its owner. Bill's dad did not have the heart to tell him that the car belonged to the pastor of the neighboring parish.

And besides the entertainment he provided for many a priest of the Diocese, he also modeled for them excellence in ministry. A priest extraordinaire for the entire length of his priesthood, he stood out from his peers in many different ways. Many a priest came to him for counsel, many saw him as a mentor, and many sought his wisdom when tangled in the web of a difficult pastoral problem. The priests of the diocese would be greatly impoverished had Bill Stanton never been born.

And this parish, our parish, would be greatly impoverished had Bill Stanton never been born. Who will ever forget Bicentennial Sunday, July 4th of 1976, when Bill celebrated his first mass here at St. Ambrose? I was on the altar with him and, though we were friends, I had never heard him preach. After he read the Gospel, I remember sitting down to listen to his sermon only to find him exiting the pulpit and heading out into the congregation. Here was this 52 year-old man running up and down the aisle as though he were on fire. He filled the church with an electricity most of us had never seen or experienced before. He spoke with such enthusiasm and conviction that even the most comatose of parishioners raised their heads in attention. A model of church and worship got set into motion that weekend and our lives have been dramatically altered for the better ever since.

Think of the way he empowered us to take charge of this parish. Think of the courage he had to raise issues and advocate for causes that weren't very popular here in South Buffalo, how he often spoke a truth few of us wished to hear. Think of how he was always there when we needed him, at our house if someone we loved died, at our bedside if we were sick, and in a chair nearby when we needed to cry. Think of the tremendous eulogies he gave for so many who had died and how so many of us hoped he'd live long enough to preach at our funerals when the day of our death arrived.

Think about how he made us laugh, how he pumped so much joy into our parish. He must have told us a thousand times how his family used to live on Roanoke Parkway but then they got a little money and moved to a place off Abbott Road. That always brought laughter no matter how often it was said. Or how about his telling us how people call me "Duke" because I came from Polish nobility. Or how about the true story of how, when John Paul II was elected Pope, I was too absorbed in making out my baseball line up to care. Speaking of Popes, my one regret is that Pope John Paul II didn't die before Bill. Bill was a student of the papacy and, whenever Papal elections were held, he was in his glory. Papers would be strewn across his desk with biographies of the Cardinals and he'd carefully handicap their chance for election with an opinion or two as to the politics of the process. I'd imagine that when the day of Pope John Paul II's death finally arrives, Bill, from his perch in heaven, will do what he can to influence the choice of his successor.

Think of how Bill both inspired us and at the same time broke our hearts as for the past two years he pushed himself to do ministry despite pain and discomfort, despite looking haggard and tired and worn, how he pushed himself to continue his commitment to say Mass and deliver outstanding homilies each and every Sunday. My God, how impoverished we here at St. Ambrose would be if Bill Stanton were never born.

And how impoverished Peg Stanton would be and Sheila and Eileen and Ellen and Maureen and Patti and John. Bill loved his family. They were his pride and joy. He loved to visit Peg on his day off even though he'd sleep in her Barcalounger for hours on end.

And finally, if Bill Stanton were never born, my life would be greatly impoverished as would be Jack Weimar's and Pat Keleher's and Jim Croglio's and Jack Connif's. Bill was more than a friend; he was a mentor, a sage, role model, a sounding board, and a giant in the priesthood. He was a Renaissance man. He helped make us who we are and brought out the best that was within us. Our lives would be terribly bereft had Bill Stanton never been born.

So when all is said and done and when you put it all together, Bill Stanton had a lot in common with the mythical George Bailey. Had he not been born, many a place would be bereft, many a life would be impoverished. Bill indeed had lived a wonderful life and not just a wonderful life, but also a saintly life, an extraordinary life, a magnificent life, an unbelievable life.

15

You might recall that at the end of the film *It's a Wonderful Life*, George Bailey's brother Harry toasted him as the "richest man in town." I toast all of you today. You are the richest people in the world because you were a part of this man's life.

The Awful Kindnesses of Others

Scripture Lesson: John 11: 1-45
"…Jesus was troubled in spirit, moved by the deepest emotions…"

A catalog of clichés employed to comfort but which in fact do more harm than good.

It's hard to believe time has gone by so quickly, but it will be 21 years this June that my dad passed away. His death wasn't at all expected. He had gone to Pittsburgh on a baseball excursion a few days earlier and on the day of his death, he went to work at our family grocery store with no evidence of any ill health. Yes, he had a heart condition, but it wasn't life threatening and there wasn't any reason to believe that he would not live to a ripe old age. He died that day of a heart attack at the age of 59.

I mention that as a bit of a backdrop for several experiences I had with people who had come to my dad's wake, fully intending to give comfort to my family and me. In what I know was an attempt to extend sympathy, in what I know was an unconscious act on their part, there were at least six individuals who shook my hand and said, "Father, it was for the best!" I'm sure they never gave a second thought to what they just said, but in essence they were telling me that it was better that my dad die than to continue to live the healthy and happy life he had been living prior to his death. Now, maybe they thought that he had suffered from a long and debilitating disease, maybe they thought he had been languishing on mechanical life supports for months on end, but you'd think they would have checked that out before suggesting that his death was "for the best." And even if the facts were different and his death did relieve him of a great deal of suffering, it could well be that my perception of what was best for my dad was for him to be alive, no matter how horrid a state "alive" happened to be.

The individuals who came to my dad's wake and said: "It was for the best!" committed a mistake far too many make when comforting those who grieve the loss of a loved one. They used a cliché, a cliché they probably heard mouthed in a similar circumstance. And, as is the case with most clichés, they transmit far more pain than comfort. I believe Ann Kaiser Stearns, who gave us that helpful book *Living Through Personal Crisis*[1], put it best when she described clichés as the "awful kindnesses of others."

With today's Gospel centering on Martha and Mary's wake for their brother Lazarus, I thought I'd talk with you today about those "awful kindnesses of others." I thought I'd talk with you about clichés in the hopes that more sensitivity will emerge in the comforting of those who grieve, that fewer will be the times when things are said better left unsaid.

Take that cliché: "It must have been God's will"! I will never forget a story told by a Lutheran colleague of a funeral he conducted one Saturday afternoon for a 26-year-old man in his congregation who had died in an automobile accident. The man was scheduled to have been married that very same afternoon. Wednesday night he went out with a few friends to celebrate and, upon leaving the restaurant, a drunk driver ran his car off the road. He died shortly thereafter. In the same church, on the same day, at about the same hour when his wedding was to have taken place, the family gathered for his funeral. He was buried in the cemetery adjacent to the church. While heading back to his office after the funeral was over, my Lutheran colleague was stopped by the man's fiancée. She said to him with tears in her eyes: "Pastor, if one more person tells me it was God's will, I am going to scream. Why are they teaching me to hate God?"

The one thing that should never be said when someone dies is that it was God's will. Never do we know enough to say that. To claim that it was God's will only helps push grieving people away from God, away from a highly important source of comfort and consolation. I've always appreciated the comments of William Sloane Coffin after his son Alex died. He died when his car accidentally veered off the road and into the Boston River. Dr. Coffin said that his consolation came in knowing that it was not the will of God that Alex died, that the truth was and that his belief was that when the waves closed over his son's sinking car God shed the first tear. God's heart ached just as surely as his own.

And then there's the cliché: "God never gives you anything you can't handle!" Harriet Schiff, who has given us several beautiful books on bereavement, wrote about her reaction to that cliché when she heard her minister use it to give comfort after her son died. "My first reaction," she wrote, "was to think it was my fault that he had died. If I had been a weaker person, God might not have taken away my son." And besides its producing guilt, there is also the matter of the cliché's inaccuracy. If God never gives us anything we can't handle, how does one account for the miscalculations: the breakdowns, the suicides that have felled more than a few unable to cope with their grief.

Then there's the other God cliché: "God took your mother away because he needed her more than you!" or worse yet: "God chose your child to be with him because God chooses only the brightest flowers to brighten heaven!" All that's heard when those clichés are spoken is that guilt is in order for our selfishness, that we should be ashamed for wanting our mother or child alive rather than in the halls of heaven. In other words, we're to be elated that they had died.

Then you have that cliché: "There must have been a reason!" You've heard me mention the name Rabbi Harold Kushner many times. His most famous book is *When Bad Things Happen to Good People*[2]. The rabbi wrote the book after his son died of a very rare disease called progeria, a disease where you age very rapidly resulting in death at a very young age. In a talk I heard him give several years back, he spoke of how someone came up to him and told him that the reason his son died was because God wanted him to write a book that was going to help millions of people. All Kushner could think of after that remark was how terrible God must be to do bad things to innocent people just so something good may enter upon the world.

We like to say: "There must have been a reason!" because it is a lot easier to be accepting of things when they follow a logical order. But the truth is that many times there is no logical reason for some bad thing to happen. To suggest that God has reasons of which we're not aware is to suggest a God in whom it might be difficult for the griever to find any sort of help or consolation.

And then you have the whole string of "Be strong!" clichés with the problem being the suggestion that the griever neither weep nor cry when it's precisely what they most need to do. My friend Dr. Tom Frantz likes to say that when we experience a loss, a huge vial of something called grief gets injected into our bodies and if we hope to heal we have to let out that grief and crying and weeping happens to provide that service. Studies have shown that there is a distinct toxic difference between tears of grief and tears of joy and so crying rids the body of toxic chemicals and in that way serves a very valuable therapeutic purpose.

Then there is the expression: "You just have to keep going!" A young widow left with three children doesn't need to hear that for she knows better than anyone that she has to keep going and a friend who has the insensitivity to tell her what she already painfully knows only furthers her distress.

There are also those "discount" clichés first and foremost of which is the expression: "It could be worse!" Whenever that's expressed, all we're doing is discounting a person's awful tragedy. We're implying, in essence that, in the suffering Olympics, they'd only win a bronze medal.

In that same category is the cliché often used to comfort a mother who has experienced a miscarriage or who has given birth to a stillborn child, the cliché being: "You can always have other children!" First of all, there are some mothers who cannot have other children. Maybe she's now too old or maybe her health is such that another pregnancy is out of the question. If that's so, you're salting an already open wound. And even if, in fact, the mom could have a dozen other children, no one can replace the child who died. That child was special and significant and unique and to say to that Mom: "you could always have other children" is tantamount to suggesting that there are plenty of "dogs" available for purchase.

And then there's that oft stated cliché: "If there's anything I can do, let me know, give me a call!" Most bereaved individuals are so distraught, so taken up by the gravity of their grief that they are in no position to be making any calls. To leave the burden of making contact upon their shoulders speaks of insensitivity and furthermore, if we really do wish to be of help, we should be doing the calling. We should be the ones checking on their welfare following the funeral.

And then there's the expression: "You'll get over it!" Our mouthing such an expression reduces the most awful tragedy in a person's life to an "it." And finally, the cliché that probably causes more anger and rage in the bereaved than any other is the cliché: "I know how you feel!"

No one knows how another person feels because we are not that person and even if we have been where they have been, we cannot know the depth of their feeling in any given circumstance any more than they can know ours.

I could go on with dozens of clichés, further examples of those "awful kindnesses of others" but it's important that I say a word on what should be our response when someone we care about experiences a loss. I believe Jesus in our Gospel today stands as our model and our guide. When he came to the wake, to the graveside of his friend Lazarus, it's recorded that he wept and that, I'm sure, did more to comfort Martha and Mary than anything else he said or did.

We best help grieving people when we let them know we care and that is done best without words. The display of our tears, the warmth generated by our hug, the loving grasp of a hand, true exhibitions of our honest feelings, really says it all. If we're genuine in our concern for the bereaved, they'll know it without the benefit of words.

RICHARD E. ZAJAC

So please, drop those clichés that you might be in the habit of employing. Abandon the notion and you need say something meaningful in order to be helpful. Don't let your honest concern be destroyed by a statement better left unsaid. Be there for that person who hurts, tell them you're sorry and if, like Jesus, you need to cry, do so without fear or embarrassment. The beautiful words of French novelist Alfred Camus captures best the feeling of the bereaved. They go as follows: "Don't walk behind me, I may not lead! Don't walk in front of me, I may not follow! Just walk beside me and be my friend."

Offenses of the Spirit

Scripture Lesson: Luke 15: 1-3, 11-32
"...He was angry and when he refused to enter the house, his father came out and pleaded with him..."

The elder son may well have hurt the father far more so than did the prodigal son.

Professor A. W. Momerie once published a provocative essay[3], provocative in the sense that it ridiculed our tendency to assume that the offenses commonly classified as crimes are the offenses which cause the greatest amount of human misery. The professor claimed instead that the highest doses of pain and suffering come from offenses for which the law makes no provisions, offenses for which there is listed no punishment or penalty. He called them "offenses of the spirit" and he described them as sins generated by temperament or mood or thought or disposition. What makes those sins particularly reprehensible is that the offender can commit them every hour of every moment of every day with impunity.

We find such an offender in the elder son of today's Gospel. Unlike his brother, he didn't leave home and participate in "loose living." He was the "good son." But if you'll note his mood and his attitude and his temperament, I'm willing to bet that it was a cause of far more grief and misery for the father than was the wayward behavior of the younger son.

I have a colleague in Rochester whose first assignment was with a pastor who was beloved by his people. He was one of the most popular priests in his diocese. The problem was that the pastor was another sort of person inside the rectory. As gregarious as he was in public, that's how "ungregarious" he was in private. He was wont to sit at the dining room table never uttering a word during the entire length of the meal. He also exhibited behind closed doors mood swings, temper tantrums, and periodic bursts of obscenities. He would also pout from time to time, which led to my friend agonizing over whether or not he was the cause of the pouting. It got to a point where my friend and colleague began experiencing health problems, that's how difficult living in that rectory had become.

When you think about it, that pastor did not commit any offense punishable by law. There's no penalty assigned for his particular behavior. His were offenses of the spirit. But let me tell you, those offenses inflicted more pain and suffering upon my colleague than would of been the case had the pastor stolen his wallet or vandalized his car or cheated him out of money, all bonafide crimes.

And then there's the pain and suffering that can come from living with or being with someone who is extremely negative, someone from whom never is heard an encouraging word.

I'm reminded of Lucy of Peanuts fame. In one memorable and not atypical strip, she's talking with her alleged friend Charlie Brown: "You, Charlie Brown, are a foul ball in the line drive of life. You're in the shadow of your own goalpost. You are a miscue. You are three puts on the 18th green. You are a 7-10 split in the 10th frame. You're a missed free throw, a shanked nine iron, a called third strike." The strip ends with Lucy asking: "Have I made myself clear?"

Not everyone is as blatant as Lucy in their negativity, but there are many who never have a good word to say, many who seem to relish uttering negative remarks. Not only is it extraordinarily difficult to live with such a person, but that person's temperament can have a deleterious effect upon any and all who might happen to come under their influence.

I was reading a piece from Dan Wakefield's book *Creating from the Spirit*[4] and it told of Judy Collins, the great singer. It told of how a high-school teacher's negative remarks about her abilities froze her from writing her songs for quite a number of years. It's also mentioned as to how a teacher's negative remark caused a famous priest from Ireland to put a damper on his academic work, to delay his education. Now Collins and that priest were lucky. They eventually overcame the negative remarks and moved on with their life. But there are many not as lucky. There are many today enduring the pain and suffering of a limited life thanks to a negative remark, thanks to an offense of the spirit.

And then you have those who may be neither negative nor moody but who inflict pain and suffering by turning off their every emotion, by walking around devoid of any affect, giving no indication whatsoever as to how they happen to be feeling.

I'm reminded of that classic science fiction movie called *The Invasion of the Body Snatchers*. The premise of the movie was that aliens had visited Earth and left behind these pods that would open to a body that exactly resembled someone in the particular town featured in the film. When that someone fell asleep, the pod body took over that life. Since the body was an exact duplicate of the person whose life it took over, it was difficult to know, as time went on, as to who was an alien and who was a real human being. The one differentiating factor discovered by the Kevin McCarthy character was that the alien showed no emotion. They didn't smile or laugh or wince or cry. As far as their emotional range was concerned, they were totally flat, giving no indication whatsoever that they were feeling anything at all.

I'm afraid to say that there are a lot of people who happen to fit that description and the sad part is that they're not an alien. They are a bonafide human being. And the fact that they show no emotion leaves you wondering and guessing as to how they truly happen to feel, wondering and guessing as to what may be going on inside them. You're left speculating as to whether they're happy or sad, content or angry, pleased or disturbed. Their "icy" temperament provides no clue. And I'm not talking here of a bad mood, I'm talking of someone deliberately choosing to be distant from others.

Once again, he or she is not doing anything punishable by law. Their activity is not listed anywhere as a crime. The fact is, however, that it torments the lives of those they're close to and near. It's another example of an offense of the spirit, another example of how someone's disposition can evoke a considerable amount of pain and suffering.

And then there are those on the opposite side of the ledger, those who readily and freely display their emotions but they do so in volatile and unpredictable ways.

The great music conductor Toscanini was as well known for his ferocious temper as he was for his outstanding skills. When members of his orchestra played badly, he would pick up anything in sight and hurl it to the floor. During one rehearsal, a flat note caused the genius to grab his valuable watch and throw it against the wall breaking it into a million pieces. Shortly thereafter, he received a gift from his devoted cast of musicians. It was a velvet-lined box containing two watches, one was a beautiful gold timepiece and the other was a cheap watch on which was inscribed: "For Rehearsals Only."

There are many people who possess a temper not unlike that of Toscanini but, unlike Toscanini, it's a temper not as finely focused nor as easily forgivable. I'm referring to those who get bothered by every little thing, those whose temper can be inflamed by the slightest of problems or difficulties or imperfections. Being in their presence requires walking on eggshells. It requires nerves of steel for the worry is constant that something will occur that will set them off.

Like those guilty of moodiness, a negative temperament, or a flat set of emotions, these individuals are constantly committing an offense of the spirit and such offenses have been known to exact more pain and suffering than many of the crimes for which people have been placed in jail

Then you have the pain and suffering that comes from the failure to listen. A little girl was watching television in her bedroom when her mother called out: "Michele come to dinner!" No response. A short time later mother called out again: "Michele come to dinner!" Again, no response. Finally the mother shouted: "Michele come to dinner!"

The little girl came bounding down the stairs and ran into the kitchen and with an innocent look on her face said: "Sorry Mom, I didn't hear you when you called me the first two times."

There are individuals who not only do not hear the first two times someone speaks to them but they do not hear anytime someone speaks to them. They're so self-centered and so self-absorbed that no attention at all is paid to what anyone has to say. Communication is a one-way street and the message is clear to those they're close to and near that how or what they think is of no relevance whatsoever. Being in their presence exacts a toll and that toll is an offense of the spirit.

Finally, there is what could well be the worst of all offenses of the spirit and that's the absence of love. There was a 35 year-long study done involving students from Harvard University. It revealed that, of the students who described their parents as loving, only 29% experienced and suffered a significant illness in the 35 years since leaving school. Of those students who did not feel love in their home, who felt an absence of love on the part of their parents, a remarkable 98 percent experienced and suffered a significant illness in the 35 years since they left school. Living in a place where love is never found is tantamount to living in hell.

So when you come right down to it, Professor Momerie was right on target. A lot more pain and suffering, the greatest amounts of human misery and, I'll add, the greatest incidences of illness; they do not come from offenses invoking a penalty. They come instead from offenses for which the law makes no provision. They would be what you'd call offenses of the spirit, sins of attitude, sins generated by temperament, mood, thought or disposition.

So in looking at today's familiar parable of the prodigal son, a case can be made for the elder son providing the father a lot more grief than the younger son. Whereas the more famous prodigal committed sins of the flesh, the less famous elder son committed sins of the spirit and I needn't tell you again as to how much more pain and suffering they happen to inflict.

So my friends, take time to see if you're guilty of an offense of the spirit, take time to see if you have a bit of the elder brother within you.

If you're like my colleague's former pastor, someone who is moody and irritable; if you're like Lucy in that Peanuts comic strip or like that teacher of Judy Collins and that Irish priest, someone who's always negative or quick with the negative remark; if you're like those aliens from the *Invasion of the Body Snatchers* and deliberately show no affect or emotion whatsoever; if you have a temper like Toscanini; if you're worse than Michele and never hear anything when someone speaks to you; if you haven't shown or provided love; it's time you mended your ways. It's time you took the lead from that prodigal son and reconciled with those you've harmed and hurt.

What's a Perfectionist to Do?

Scripture Lesson: Mark 6:7-13
"…If anyplace will not receive you or hear you, shake its dust from your feet…"

A guide to helping a perfectionist cope with imperfection.

I don't know how many of you are familiar with Belleek China but it's arguably the best china money can buy. The reason for its positive reputation rests in its method of quality control. Every piece of china the Belleek Company produces is held up to an enormously bright light where it's examined and scrutinized for imperfection. Should the slightest flaw be detected; the cup or the plate or whatever is being examined is immediately destroyed. As far as the Belleek China Company is concerned, if it's not perfect, it's not worthy of the Belleek name. The makers of Waterford Crystal employ that same philosophy, that same method of quality control. When it comes to Belleek China and Waterford Crystal, there are no such things as seconds because neither company tolerates imperfection.

One of the problems that often occurs is that we will treat life like Belleek treats its china. We will look at life the way Waterford looks at its crystal. We expect things to be perfect. We want things to be perfect. We demand things to be perfect. And the sad truth is that life is neither like china nor like crystal. The sad truth is that life is not capable of being perfect. Immanuel Kant, I believe, put it best when he said: "Out of timber as crooked as that which life is made of, nothing perfectly straight can be carved."

That being said, what's a perfectionist to do? How's a perfectionist to cope with the truth of imperfection? Well, first of all, he or she needs to realize that what they've been pursuing is beyond the scope of human power. It's something reserved for God and God alone.

When the famed sculptor Gutzan Borglum was working on Mount Rushmore, he was asked if he thought his artwork was perfect in every detail. He looked up at the towering face of George Washington that roughly took up the space of a five-story building. He studied it for a while and then said: "Not today!" Washington's nose is about one inch too long. But if you come back in 10,000 years, erosion being what it is, it'll probably be perfect then. Borglun was, of course, being facetious. The truth is that Mt. Rushmore will never be perfect because perfection lies beyond human reach.

Orthodox Jews always leave a small patch unpainted in a freshly painted room because they believe to be perfect is not of this world. Weavers of Oriental rugs believe much the same thing and so they'll always leave one stitch undone in every rug they sew. So perfectionists need to realize, first and foremost, that perfection is reserved for God, that perfection is beyond the scope of human power.

And they also need to realize that imperfection is fundamental to life. One of the most interesting essays I've ever read was entitled *Mistress of the Margin*[5]. It was written by one of my favorite authors F.W. Boreham. He applied that title to nature and went on to point out how nature factors into its work a substantial margin for error. Nature, he wrote, will want a bird to enter into life so a dozen will be hatched with nature knowing perfectly well that 11 of the 12 are merely margin. They will fall victim to the foxes and the weasels and the snakes, leaving one to fulfill its destiny as a bird. Nature, wrote Boreham, wants a tree so she'll plant a hundred with 99 of those hundred being margin. They'll be mowed down or eaten by the cattle or destroyed by the sheep or the deer or the fox, thus leaving one tree to fulfill its destiny as a tree. Boreham went on to write as to how the ovary of a codfish contains nearly 10 million eggs and if each of those eggs would produce fish that would survive until maturity, the entire ocean would be packed solid with that single species of fish. What will in fact happen is that larger fish will feast on the major portion of those 10 million eggs leaving but a few to make it to maturity. They're merely a part of nature's margin for error

That essay, in essence, told of how imperfection is fundamental to nature, how nature in its grand design factors in a wide margin for error, factors in a wide margin for imperfection. If that were not so, if it weren't for imperfection, this planet would be so filled with plants and animals that there would be little if any room for human life.

The third thing a perfectionist needs to consider in light of imperfection is the fact that imperfection has served as the basis for the quality of life we presently enjoy. James Watts, the inventor of the steam engine, once declared that what is most wanted in mechanical engineering is a history of failures. We want, he said, a "book of blots." John Hunter, the eminent Scottish surgeon, used to say that medical science will only progress when professionals gain the courage to publish their failures as well as their successes. Down through the centuries, it's been the failures, it's been the imperfections that have given birth to the advances in science and technology that has made life far more comfortable than it once had been; it's been the failures, it's been the imperfections that have given birth to so many of the inventions and medicines and surgical procedures that has made our illnesses and physical deficiencies much easier to bear and to handle. One could say that imperfections are responsible for the quality of life we presently enjoy.

The fourth thing a perfectionist needs to do with the impossibility of perfection is to consider how perfection can ruin fun, how being perfect could well take the joy out of much of what we may happen to do. I remember a friend telling the hypothetical story about a talented baseball player. As a batter, he was phenomenal. He would always get a hit and every hit, a home run. As a pitcher, he was equally phenomenal. He struck out every batter he faced. The problem he had was that no one wanted to play baseball with him. He was too perfect.

Back in my coaching days, I never liked to play a team we could defeat at will. It usually meant that often during the course of a game I'd have to have a batter intentionally bunt a ball back to the pitcher just so we could make the out necessary to end a very long inning in which many runs were scored. Now I'm not trying to say that my team was perfect but we were much closer to perfection than the other team and that made for a very boring game and a very unsatisfying victory.

I believe that is what's taken much of the luster off the Olympic Games. Several years back, a decision was made by the United States to allow the professionals and not the amateurs to represent the country in Olympic competition. The result was watching Michael Jordan and company roll over their basketball opponents at will making it a hollow victory at best. I failed to see how they could be proud of those Gold Medals which they barely broke a sweat to achieve. When it comes to recreation, when it comes to sport, when it comes to any sort of competition perfection can often result in the absence of any fun or satisfaction.

The fifth thing a perfectionist needs to do with the impossibility of perfection is to consider that good people, saintly people, great people are often far from perfect. I recently read a biography of Joseph De Veuster, otherwise known as Father Damian. The son of a Belgian farmer, he joined the Society of the Sacred Heart of Jesus and Mary and became a missionary to the Pacific Islands in 1863. Ordained in Honolulu, he volunteered nine years later to take charge of a settlement of lepers, which the Hawaiian government had deported to a remote island. Upon arriving on that island, he found little running water and lepers living in vermin-infested huts. They had been given little if any medical care and their food supply hardly met their needs. Father Damian took that island by storm and turned it from a hell into a heaven. Almost single-handedly, he ministered to the physical and spiritual needs of over 600 lepers over the course of 16 years and in turn he inspired others to follow in his footsteps so that his work would continue long after he was gone. He would, himself, in the end, fall victim to leprosy and later die from that very disease. I don't believe there's any question in anybody's mind that this man was qualified to be a saint. John Paul II declared him one in 1995.

My reason for referencing the Father Damian story is that it's a story of someone who was anything but perfect. It's been said, for an example, that he could be domineering as well as indiscreet. At times, it was reported that he could be narrow-minded and at times he could be bigoted. His superiors rebuked him on more than a few occasions for boorish behavior. He was tabbed as being testy and irritable and "hygienically challenged." Father Damian was a saintly man but he was not a perfect man.

And I'm sure if you probed the biographies of other saints, you'd find the thread of imperfection running through them as well. There are no perfect people but there are beautiful people and saintly people and extraordinary people, and the fact they're not perfect does not take anything away from their beauty or their saintliness or their extraordinariness.

So how's a perfectionist supposed to deal with the reality of imperfections? First, he or she needs to realize that perfection is reserved for God. Second, they're to realize that imperfection is fundamental to life. Third, they're to realize that imperfection is responsible for their quality of life. Fourth, they're to realize that perfection makes for no fun and little, if any, satisfaction. Fifth, they're to realize that imperfection does not diminish people's greatness. And sixth, they're to realize that being perfect could well result in their missing out on a whole lot of life.

In the early days of our country, a Native American princess went to visit a neighboring tribe that was known far and wide for its magnificent cornfields. The corn, which they produced at harvest time, was extraordinary. Upon completing her visit, the princess asked if she might select one ear of their corn so she might use its seeds for her own tribe's cornfields. Graciously, her request was granted but there was one stipulation. She was to walk down but one row of corn. She could choose any ear of corn she wanted, but could not turn back to pick an ear she had already passed. So, she began walking slowly down the row looking intently for that one perfect ear of corn. She walked and looked and pondered and studied but could not bring herself to pick one single ear fearing that a better one might be found further ahead. All of a sudden, before she knew it, she had walked beyond the designated row of corn. Since there was no turning back, her pursuit of that perfect ear resulted in her going home empty-handed.

That's a great parable for perfectionists. If a perfectionist waits for the perfect date to come along, he or she may find himself or herself never going out at all. If a perfectionist waits for the perfect job to appear, he or she may be forever unemployed. If a perfectionist waits for that perfect situation, that perfect moment to do what they want and need to do, he or she may well discover that their waiting has resulted in their growing too old or it being too late for them to do it. Like that Native American princess, the perfectionist will have come to find that they've walked out of the field of life empty-handed. G. K. Chesterton once said that anything worth doing is worth doing poorly, which means that we oughtn't wait for things to be perfect to do what should or what needs to be done.

And then, finally, when it comes to the reality of imperfection, perfectionists should come to realize that imperfection does not stand in the way of God's love. I'm reminded here of that scene from Godspell where Jesus is with his disciples in the upper room. He takes a bucket of water, a rag, and a mirror and he goes to his disciples one by one and washes away their painted faces. Then he holds up a mirror in front of them so they can see themselves as they really are. And then he hugs them. The point is clear. We don't have to hide our imperfections. God loves us just the way we are! God loves us warts and all.

Jesus in our Gospel was speaking to the perfectionists amongst his disciples. He's telling them not to expect perfection in their work, that failure will be inevitable. And upon meeting with failure and imperfection, all they need do is shake the dust from their feet and move on. Jesus was, in essence, reminding his disciples of the fact of the reality of imperfection.

So to all of you perfectionists: Don't despair as to the reality of imperfections! Remember why the Orthodox Jews leave a patch of a newly painted room unpainted. Consider what the planet would be like if nature worked perfectly. Think of what imperfection has taught scientists and inventors and doctors. Think of the fun and satisfaction which would be lost if things were perfect. Remember that saints aren't perfect. Recall how the wait for perfection can result in our going home empty-handed. Consider the fact that God loves us warts and all! That unlike the Belleek China and the Waterford Crystal companies, God tolerates our imperfections and holds us special even though in the big picture of life, we'd be lucky to pass as seconds.

Is Your Halo on Too Tight?

Scripture Lesson: Luke 18: 9-14
"…I give you thanks O God that I am not like the rest of men…"

Contrary to popular opinion, there's no such thing as a sinless life.

Bishop Fulton Sheen once told the story of a self-righteous individual who went to see his physician complaining of a headache. The doctor, upon his examination, asked him if he felt any pain at all in his forehead. The patient responded: "Yes I do!"

"How about a throbbing pain in the back of the head?" The patient nodded his head in the affirmative. "And do you have a piercing pain at the side of your temples?"

The patient said, "Yes, doctor, I have that as well."

"In that case," said the doctor, "I know exactly what your problem is! Your halo is on too tight!"

I tell that story because I believe too many people think they have a halo. Too many people have this notion that they are leading a life free of sin. And I say that because when the topic of confession arises in any of my conversations with Catholics, many if not all will claim they no longer frequent the sacrament because they really can't think of anything to confess. With that in mind, I thought I'd take some time today to talk with you about why people believe they have a halo, why people believe that they happen to be without sin.

Well, first of all, it's because they assume that their blessed lives are a testimony to their sinlessness. Sometime ago, a Dennis the Menace cartoon portrayed Dennis walking away from the Wilson home with his friend and sidekick Joey. Both boys had a hand full of cookies and Joey asked Dennis, "I wonder what we did to deserve this?" Dennis gave a wonderful answer. He said, "Look Joey, Mrs. Wilson gave us those cookies not because we're nice but because she's nice."

If we have found our lives to be filled with many blessings, it's because God has been nice enough to make those blessings available for us to have. And that availability comes by way of God's goodness and generosity and that goodness and generosity is available to the bad as well as to the good. So if we believe that we are without sin because of the many blessings that have filled our lives, we need to defer to the wisdom of Dennis the Menace. Those blessings are there not because we are nice but because God is nice.

A second reason why people believe they are without sin is that they habitually make adverse comparisons. A woman was riding a train and she suddenly caught sight of a white cottage on a hillside. Against the backdrop of the dark green grass, the cottage sparkled in the sun. It was a lovely and beautiful sight. Months later, the same woman was on the same train. Now it was winter and snow covered the ground. The woman remembered the cottage and watched for it. This time she was shocked. Against the backdrop of the sparkling snow, the cottage looked dirty and tattered and drab.

All too often we form an opinion of ourselves based on adverse comparisons. We look at ourselves against the backdrop of dark green grass instead of against the backdrop of white snow. In other words, we do as that Pharisee did in today's Gospel, we compare ourselves to some notorious sinner instead of comparing ourselves to some notorious saint.

There's a wonderful anecdote involving famed golfer Bobby Jones. Once in a national championship, he drove the ball into the woods. He went after it alone and while standing by the ball, he accidentally grazed it. He then struck the ball with his club and it bounded on to the fairway When he came out of the woods, he signaled to the tournament officials and when they came by, he told them he was penalizing himself one stroke for having accidentally grazed his golf ball. He would end up losing that national championship by one stroke. Shortly thereafter, he was praised to high heaven for his honesty and sportsmanship regarding that incident in the woods. He waved it off, he wouldn't accept it. "If you praise me for that," he said, "you might as well praise the person next to you for not having robbed a bank!"

Many people believe they are without sin because they are not like the person in jail. They haven't robbed a bank. They haven't raped anybody. They didn't kill their next-door neighbor. By making such adverse comparisons, it's no wonder that they feel so good about themselves. It's no wonder how they've been led to believe that they are without sin. Standing next to someone who's committed some horrendous sin or some heinous crime, they appear quite saintly.

And that brings me to the third reason why people believe they are without sin and that's because they look at sin from only one side of a ledger. They look at what they did instead of also looking at what they failed to do.

Sir John Robert Seeley was a historian and writer who lived in the latter part of the 19th century. In one of his books, he pointed at the radical difference between the villains featured in the parables of Jesus and the villains featured in most of literature. In the typical novel, the villain does something definitely wrong, the villain does what he/she ought not to have done. In the stories that Jesus told, the villain doesn't really do anything wrong, the villain merely doesn't do what he or she ought to have done.

There's the priest and the Levite who passed by on the other side of the man lying at the side of the road. Then, there's that rich man who allowed the beggar Lazarus to lay unhelped at his doorstep. Then you have that servant who took the talent entrusted to him and hid it in the ground. And then there was a hired hand who did only what it was his duty to do. The villains in Christ's parables, the sinners he so frequently denounces are not the people who violate the 10 Commandments.

They are not the people who participated in some obvious wrongful action. Instead, they're the people who fail to love, they're the people who could have done something positive and magnanimous but instead did nothing and all.

When you come right down to it, in the eyes of Jesus, what we failed to do is just as, if not more sinful than what we did. In the overall picture of one's life, many can look at a copy of the 10 Commandments and proudly say that they haven't violated any of them. But I'm not so sure that there are many who can look at the parables of Jesus and proudly say that they did what those villains in the parables failed to do. In all too many cases, it's the not looking at the "failed to do" side of sin's ledger that leads us to believe that we are without sin.

The fourth reason why people believe they are without sin is the inability to see. I heard of a woman and her daughter who went Christmas shopping together. The crowds were awful. The woman had to skip lunch because she was on a tight schedule. She became tired and hungry and her feet were hurting. She was more than a little irritable. As they left the last store, she asked her daughter, "Did you see the nasty look the salesman gave me?" The daughter looked at her and said, "Mom, he didn't give it to you. You had it when you walked in!"

Many times, what's bothersome to us when it comes to others is what's bothersome to them when it comes to us. Many times we see a sin in another person's life precisely because it's fairly prominent in our own. And if we don't have a daughter calling it to our attention, then chances are good that we suffer from an eye ailment common to many. We can see clearly the sins of others but we do not see clearly the sins of our own. And it's because of that impaired vision that we can make the claim that we are without sin.

The fifth reason why people believe they are without sin is that they've gotten pretty adept at excusing away their bad behavior. When Abraham Lincoln was president, there was a particular man who always seemed to be up to no good, who always got himself into trouble. And whenever he was admonished for his bad behavior, he always said that he couldn't help himself, that he wasn't able to resist certain urges inside him. When Abraham Lincoln got wind of his excuse, he is quoted as saying: "That man's got a bad case of the 'can't help its'!"

Many a sinner has a bad case of the "can't help its." And so in their eyes they're not really guilty of the sins they committed and, being thus absolved from bad behavior, have no trouble claiming a life without sin. And if they don't have the "can't help its" to absolve their behavior, there's always the passing on of the blame and the responsibility onto someone else's shoulders.

Some of you might recall the story of John Steinbeck's sharecropper. He wanted to know who foreclosed on his farm. He went to the local banker. The banker said he wasn't the guilty party. It was the home office that did it. He goes to the home office and they said they weren't the guilty party. It was the board of directors who did it. He goes to the board of directors. They said they weren't the guilty party. It was the stockholders who did it. The conclusion was that nobody was guilty when the truth of the matter was that everybody was guilty.

If one can't excuse sin by reason of helplessness, one can always excuse sin by reason of responsibility, by reason of the fact that someone or something other than themselves are the guilty party. Many have made the claim of a sinless life because they've successfully excused away any and all bad behavior leaving no sin at all for which they might be guilty.

The sixth and final reason why people believe they are without sin is that the truth of the reality of their sin hasn't as yet entered their consciousness. Clarence Edward Macartney, in one of his books, tells the tale of an army officer in India who had a tiger cub as a pet. The cub was an affectionate and playful animal and was often at the side of its master. In time, it grew to its full size and strength. One day the officer was sitting in his library reading. As he read, he fell asleep. The young tiger, lying at his master's chair, began to lick his hand. There was a slight abrasion on that hand and, as the tiger licked the wound, he tasted blood. With the taste of blood, he became more and more ferocious. The officer suddenly awakened only to find himself looking straight into the eyes, not of a playful tiger cub, but looking straight into the eyes of a ferocious beast that had tasted his blood and wanted more. The officer quickly reached for his pistol and shot him dead.

Many a sin, many a wrongful relationship, will at first glance appear fairly harmless. It may even begin to become delightful and enjoyable, leading us to believe that it's not really a sin, that it's not really wrong. So we'll make the claim of a sinless life based on the fact that the truth of our sin has not as yet hit home. But as was the case with that playful cub, our sin will eventually show its true colors and its ferocity may destroy our life.

Although today's Gospel doesn't say so, I'll bet that that self-righteous Pharisee had a headache from time to time. And if he went to a doctor, I'll bet that doctor would inform him that his headache came because his halo was on too tight. My friends, if that's your problem, if you're one of those people who believe they are without sin, if you believe you have a halo, let me have you consider a few things.

First of all, consider the wisdom of Dennis the Menace. Your blessed life comes not from your being nice but from God being nice. Second, consider the backdrop for your self-analysis. Is that backdrop the life of a notorious sinner or is that backdrop the life of a notorious saint? Third, consider checking on the "failed to do" side of sin's ledger. Fourth, consider your eyesight. Do you see well the sins of others to the detriment of your own? Fifth, consider your excuses. Is it really true you couldn't help it? Is it really true you weren't guilty? And, finally, consider if that playful cub that doesn't seem sinful is not in fact a ferocious tiger. My friends get rid of your halo! It's something reserved for someone who truly happens to be without sin.

A Tonic of Huge and Big Things

Scripture Lesson: 1 Corinthians 10: 16-17
"…We, though many, are one body…"

The ways and means of a healthier, better, and fuller life.

The Fuccillo Chevrolet dealership has embarked on an advertising campaign that has taken all of Western New York by storm. It seems like almost every hour of the day, you're seeing or hearing its owner, Billy Fuccillo, in conversation with a reporter extolling the fantastic deals he's offering to anyone wishing to buy a new or used car. Each commercial ends with Billy Fucillo emphasizing how large a deal or discount a customer can expect. He sums it up in one word and we all know the word and that word is: "Huge!"

It's huge things which I'd like to talk with you about today. It's big things I'd like to discuss with you today. Huge things have been known to have healing properties. Big things have been known to possess curative powers. Bear with me as I review how big and huge things can serve as a tonic for what may happen to be ailing an individual's life.

There was a book written many years ago entitled *The Rosary*[6]. The heroine of that best seller was the Honorable Jane Chapman who had come upon hard times, her nerves having gotten the best of her. A Dr. Deryck Brand came upon the scene. When he saw how frayed her nerves had become, he immediately wrote a prescription. The prescription read: "See a few big things!" What the doctor wanted her to do was to go and see Niagara Falls or go and see the pyramids of Egypt or the skyscrapers of New York City. It was his belief that her coming face-to-face with such immense creations would cause her to realize just how small and minor were the worries that had so upset her life.

Now lest we think that the stuff of fiction, the truth is that the prescription which Dr. Deryck Brand had written was commonly written by doctors not that many years ago and it did prove to be a cure for many heavily absorbed in worries and matters that were too tiny and too small to deserve the attention they happened to be receiving. So you might say, first off, that huge things, that big things can serve as a tonic for nerves strained by life's many minor irritations, a tonic for a life bothered and harassed by worries.

And then you have huge and big things serving as a tonic for a dull and boring life. There is a lovely poem written by Edgar Frank and it's entitled "Goshen." It goes as follows:

"How can you live in Goshen?"
Said a friend from afar,
"This wretched country town
Where folks talk little things all year,
And plant their cabbage by the moon!"
Said I:
I do not live in Goshen,
I eat here, sleep here, work here;
I live in Greece,
Where Plato taught,
And Phidias carved,
And Epictetus wrote.
I dwell in Italy,
Where Michelangelo wrought
In color, form and mass;
Where Cicero penned immortal lines,
And Dante sang undying songs.

RICHARD E. ZAJAC

Think not my life is small
Because you see a puny place;
I have my books; I have my dreams;
A thousand souls have left for me
Enchantment that transcends
Both time and place.
And so I live in Paradise,
Not here.

Edgar Frank in that poem was referencing the fact that there are a lot of people from the world of art and literature who have produced unbelievable creations of mind and heart and canvas and stone and those creations can lift just about anyone out of the ordinariness of life, catapulting more than a few to the heavens above.

So if, in fact, there is anyone who feels trapped in a stifling and boring environment like Goshen; there is available to them the tonic of big things, there is available to them the tonic of huge things and that particular tonic comes not in the form of bodies of water or pyramids or skyscrapers; it comes instead in the form of the sculptures of Michelangelo, the writings of Cicero, the paintings of Da Vinci. It comes instead in the masterful creations of gifted and talented and renowned artists and composers and musicians.

And if your affliction happens to be a small and stunted life, the tonic of big and huge things can do wonders for that as well. John Maxwell in one of his books tells us something quite interesting about sharks, those fierce creatures of the deep blue sea. He tells us that sharks only grow as large as their surroundings permit. If they're caught when they're small and placed, let's say, in an aquarium, they'll adapt to that environment. They'll stay their whole lives at the size proportionate to the aquarium they happen to be in. So sharks can be as little as six inches long and yet be fully mature. Now if you were to take that same six-inch shark and let it out into the ocean, it will grow to its normal dimensions, which may be 500 times the size it was in that aquarium.

44

There are many individuals who have shark's blood yet live in an aquarium. Many individuals who are loaded with potential yet are not realizing any of that potential. For them, there is available a tonic that can get them into the ocean where they belong, to get them to realize the multiple gifts and talents that happen to lie within them. There was a novel written some years ago entitled *Second Growth*[7] and it dealt with life in a small town in Vermont, a town which afforded little in the way of opportunity for the young people living there. It happened that a good teacher took an interest in a young student filled with all kinds of promise and potential. He said to him, "Look son, if I were you, I'd take any chance I could get to go to college. There's not much else we can offer you or teach you around here and, if you don't go to college, you're going to stay the same size all your life."

Higher education is one of the big and huge things that may well serve as a tonic for a small and stunted life, a tonic for a life loaded with potential but with little to show for that potential. It behooves us to not let fear or self-doubt or a lack of opportunity make it unavailable for those who need to drink it, for those sharks amongst us for whom it would be a shame if they stay their same small size all their life.

And then you have those afflicted with what you might call a dying life. A tonic of big and huge things can be a help and aid for them as well. I love the story often told of a man hiking in the mountains who is suddenly overtaken by a snowstorm that causes him to lose his way. He knew he needed to find shelter fast or he would freeze to death. Panic stricken and with hand and feet quickly going numb, he staggered forward only find himself tripping over another man who was lying in the snow and near death. The hiker had to make a decision. Should he help the man or should he continue on in hopes of saving himself? He decides to help the man. He threw off his wet clothes, and knelt beside the man and began massaging his arms and legs. After the hiker had worked for a few minutes, the man began to respond and soon thereafter was able to get on his feet. Together the two men, supporting each other, found help.

The hiker was later informed that by helping that other man, he helped and saved himself. His massaging that stranger's arms and legs got the numbness to leave his own hands and feet. His heightened activity improved his circulation and helped bring needed warmth to his freezing body. You could say that his act of unselfishness kept him from dying.

That story is a tale of bigness. It could be said that it was big of that hiker to forgo saving his own life for the sake of that man lying in the snow. That sort of bigness is what can serve as a tonic for a dying life. Many a man dying in spirit, many woman dying in grief, many an individual dying from a listless life has been saved by acts of unselfishness, has been saved by their involving themselves in something that was bigger than they were.

I'm reminded here of that oft told statement of Dr. Alfred Adler where he claimed he could cure depression in 14 days by having the patient each day cross over the railroad tracks into the next city and there find someone in need and then proceed to address that need. One could well say that relief for dying lives, relief for listless lives can be had by drinking the tonic of big and huge things, those big and huge things being their involvement in that which it would be big of them to do.

That same tonic with those same ingredients can also serve as a pick me up, an elixir for a life that isn't dying but which happens to be in dire need of a lift. I'm thinking here of the great story of George Herbert, the famed musician and poet and saint. He was to be a part of what we would call today a "jam session," an evening of making music with other gifted musicians. It was a chance for him to play his flute, something he loved to do. On his way to Salisbury, England, where the jam session was to take place, he came upon an old man whose pony cart was broken down and in need of considerable repair. At once, George Herbert dismounted his horse, took off his coat and did what he could to help him. Several hours went by, at the end of which, the pony cart was fixed and the old man was back on the road.

When George Herbert arrived at Salisbury, his friends were astonished to behold his soiled clothes and his filthy boots and even more astounded that he arrived too late to play in the jam session and they knew how much he wanted to play his flute. They said to him: "George, you missed the music!"

"That maybe so," he said, "but as a result of what I've just done, I'll have songs at midnight."

Having done what it was big of him to do, George Herbert's heart beamed with satisfaction and pride. He'd go to bed that night pleased as punch to have been a source of help to someone in need. Not only do dying lives benefit from the tonic of big and huge things, but so do lives whose pulse is weak, lives in dire need of a lift. The tonic could well provide for them songs at midnight, the tonic could well provide for them the benefit of the pride and joy that comes from doing or having done what it would be beautiful of them to do.

So big things, huge things can be a tonic for a nerve-filled life; it can be a tonic for a dull and boring life; it can be a tonic for a small and stunted life; it can be a tonic for a dying life; a tonic for a listless life; and it can also be a tonic for an insignificant life.

I heard someone recently make the case as to why the mere fact that we are alive and breathing carries with it one tremendous legacy. That someone asked us to consider how we, for the most part, have two parents and how each of them had two parents which means we had four grandparents. Those grandparents each had two parents which means we had eight great grandparents. Counting their parents means we had 16 great great grandparents. And counting their parents, 32 great great great grandparents. And if we pursue that down through the centuries, allowing an average of 25 years between generations, that would mean that over the course of 500 years, 1,048,576 people have been involved in producing our little life.

Now if you couple that with the teachers who taught us, the farmers who raised the food we ate, the doctors and dentists who cared for our bodies and teeth, the authors who wrote the books we've read, the seamstresses who sewed the clothes we've worn, you're looking at another couple hundred people also involved in our production. And then on top of that, there is today's feast of Corpus Christi which tells us that we have been marked as a child of God, a brother or sister to Christ. You're looking at the fact that there's no way that we're insignificant! There's no way our life is unimportant! There is no way that we're not special and unique and of value! With millions involved in our making and hundreds involved in our nurturing and God overseeing it all, we're the product of an unbelievable legacy and much is expected of us.

So, my friends, if your nerves are a bit frayed by life's minor irritations, if your life is boring and dull, if you're leading a small and stunted life, if your spirit is dying, if you feel insignificant, and even if there's nothing really wrong with your life, drink the tonic of big and huge things. See Niagara Falls or the pyramids; pursue higher education; read Cicero or observe the works of Michelangelo or Da Vinci, be like that hiker and do what it would be big of you to do; do what you know will bring songs at midnight; think of the millions involved in your making; consider the fact that you're a child of God. Take that tonic and you'll be surprised by the results. You'll be in touch with the many blessings of God and those blessings are: "Huge!!!!!"

Three-O'clock-in-the-Morning Courage

Scripture Lesson: Isaiah 50: 4c-9a
"...I have set my face like flint..."

Practitioners of real courage seldom get the recognition they deserve.

On the night before the famous Battle of Waterloo, the Duke of Wellington, the leader of the English army, got little sleep. His stomach was queasy and his knees literally shook in fear. He wasn't sure he was up for the battle that would begin at morning light. When the sun began to rise, the Duke of Wellington put on his uniform, went out and rallied his troops and by day's end the course of European history changed. Napoleon was defeated. When someone asked him what it took to prevail over the enemy, he said it took an immense amount of courage. In particular, he said, it took three-o'clock-in-the-morning courage.

It's three-o'clock-in-the-morning courage that I'd like to talk with you about today. In particular, I'd like to discuss the courage mustered when fear is at its worst, when doubt is at its strongest, when despair looms heavy in the air, and when our knees are shaking so badly that we can hardly walk.

I thought Harper Lee captured that courage best in the person of Mrs. Dubose, a character in her novel *To Kill a Mockingbird*[8]. She was dying of cancer and was on heavy doses of morphine and she chose to stop the morphine so she could die, in her words, "beholdin' to nothing and to nobody." So each day she was in tremendous pain yet she didn't complain and she hung on to life with tremendous grit and determination. Atticus Finch, the lead character of the novel, made it a point to have his son Jem read to her every day and he did so because he wanted Jem to see what real courage was about. And when death would claim her life, Atticus referred to her as the bravest person he had ever known.

Three-o'clock-in-the-morning courage is not the kind they issue medals for. It's not the kind that adorns the front pages of our newspapers. You will not find it discussed on *Dateline* or on *20/20*. But it speaks volumes for strength and valor and nobility and gallantry. It is of a caliber that often makes the more popular and more external versions of courage pale by comparison.

Some years ago, there was a funeral up in Arlington National Cemetery. A young Army sergeant, a father of three children, was being buried. The man had fought in Vietnam and in the heat of battle he threw himself on a live grenade, absorbing the full impact of the blast and did so to save the lives of the soldiers who were in his company. For that act of bravery, he was posthumously awarded the Medal of Honor. His young widow came up to receive the medal from the President, the tears running down her face. As he handed her the medal, the President cited her for her bravery. He cited her for her courageously facing the challenge of raising her three children all by herself. That young widow, unlike her husband, wasn't a candidate for the Medal of Honor. But if they gave medals for three-o'clock-in-the-morning courage, she was most certainly a candidate.

I'm reminded of the mother who was seen pushing her wheelchair-bound son through the park. The young man, who appeared to be in his late teens and suffering from cerebral palsy, was leaning out of his chair taking in all the sights. You could tell that it wasn't easy for that mother to negotiate all the hills and curves but negotiate them she did, all the while talking to her son and making sure all his needs and wants were being met. Like that mother with three children, she was exhibiting three-o'clock-in-the-morning courage. There are many like that widow and like that mother of that wheelchair-bound son. There are many Mrs. Duboses gritting their way through life. They are those individuals who have had life deliver them a terrible blow, individuals who now lead a life demanding of them sacrifices of a huge nature, leading a life with burdens demanding of them all of their time and all of their energy and all of their strength and all of their freedom. They are those of whom not a day goes by when they don't wonder if they can hang on, when they don't wonder if they're up to facing another day, when they don't wonder if they can handle the stress and challenge which their children or their disease or their burdens present them. Yet carry on they do, with many exhibitions of three-o'clock-in-the-morning courage.

And then you have those who have every reason, every excuse to quit what they happen to be doing, whom no one would blame for putting a stop to what it is they are trying to accomplish yet carry-on they do, exhibiting as well tremendous amounts of three-o'clock-in-the-morning courage.

There is a beautiful statue in Mexico that bears the unusual title "In Spite Of." The name was chosen to honor the sculptor rather than the subject carved in stone. It happened that the sculptor had suffered an accident in the midst of his creating the statue and that accident resulted in the loss of his right hand. The man was so determined to finish his creation that he learned to chisel with his left hand. So the statue was entitled "In Spite Of" because in spite of his handicap the sculptor completed his work.

And so it has gone with many who have graced the world with their talents and abilities. In spite of blindness, Milton wrote. In spite of deafness, Beethoven composed. In spite of blindness and deafness, Helen Keller gave motivational speeches. In spite of rheumatic hands, Renoir painted. In spite of being blind, deaf, crippled, old, arthritic, poor, persecuted, and uneducated, people have overcome and have excelled; they have accomplished and have triumphed thanks in no small measure to their three o'clock in the morning courage. They kept on keeping on despite every reason not to.

And then there are those men and those women who tell the truth and stand by the truth when everyone else has bought into or given in to the lie. Benno Mullen Hall, a professor at the University of Cologne, tells how one morning in high school he stood last in a line of 40 students in the school yard. Their physics teacher had set up a telescope so that the students could view a planet and its various moons. The first student stepped up to the telescope and looked through it. The teacher asked if he could see anything and the boy said, "No!" But catching this disgusted and despairing look on his teacher's face, the student stammered and stuttered and then confessed to poor eyesight. The teacher hollered to him to adjust the dial near the lens. He did so and proclaimed to the teacher that he could see the planet as well as its moons. One by one, the students stepped-up to the telescope and saw what they were supposed to see. Finally, the second to last student looked into the telescope and announced that he couldn't see anything only to have the teacher holler to adjust the lens. He did so but still confessed that he couldn't see anything. The teacher, now totally disgusted, marched up to the telescope and looked in the lens and then looked up with this strange expression on his face. He had come to find that the dark cap still covered the telescopic lens. None of the students had been able to see anything at all.

That schoolyard anecdote demonstrates how many find it difficult to tell the truth or to admit to something when it's clear that it will not be well received. In general, it's easier to tell a lie than it is to tell the truth especially when the truth requires our standing alone, especially when there are consequences attached to our telling it.

G. K. Chesterton, in his autobiography, wrote of an incident in his childhood that he would never forget. His father Edward had prospered so much that he won the esteem of the community and that prompted his being elected as a trustee of the church. When word reached his mother, she protested against his father accepting the position. She exclaimed very passionately, "Oh, Edward, if you accept that, we will become respectable. We've never been respectable. Let's not begin now!"

Being true to ourself and true to our faith and true to our principles can often put us in a difficult position in terms of the community in which we live. It can put us in a difficult position in regards to our social respectability. It takes an enormous amount of courage to stand by an unpopular truth especially one which can negatively effect our status in the community. It's the kind of courage that makes for sleepless nights and queasy stomachs. It's the kind of courage that has us constantly asking ourselves as to whether or not we wouldn't have been better off going along with the lie. It's the three-o'clock-in-the-morning courage that the Duke of Wellington had so aptly defined.

And then there are those who swim against the tide trying to make a difference with little if anything to show for their efforts. I'm reminded of the scene from the classic Frank Capra film *Mr. Smith goes to Washington*. James Stewart, who played Mr. Smith, had just been elected to the U.S. Senate and just as he's about to depart for Washington, his father sits him down for a father and son chat. He tells him something the Stewart character would never forget. He tells him: "Son, just remember, it is the lost causes that are the only ones worth fighting for." And who will ever forget that scene later in the movie where Stewart is engaged in a one-man filibuster for a cause that no other member of the Senate deemed worthy enough to support.

There are many people fighting for lost causes, fighting on behalf of people about whom no one really cares, fighting to end an injustice everyone's come to accept, fighting to pump hope and life into a neighborhood everyone has given up for lost, fighting to erase a prejudice from which no one is willing to part, fighting on behalf of an ideal no one seems to hold. And they are tired and burned out and it's taxing every ounce of their energy and strength. As despair looms heavy in the air, they ask themselves each and every day the worthwhileness of continuing but continue they do. And they continue, compliments of their three-o'clock-in-the-morning courage, compliments of the bravery imbedded within their hearts.

And then finally you have those plain and ordinary folk working the corners of human life. I'm reminded here of the oft-told story of the man who witnessed this gentle soul cleaning feces off a vagrant who wandered into a homeless shelter. The man said to that gentle soul that he wouldn't do that for a million dollars and that gentle soul said in reply: "Neither would I!"

There are many out there doing what that gentle soul was doing and for little pay. There are many out there ministering to people in roach- and rat-infested houses, ministering to people in neighborhoods where gunfire rings out on a daily basis. There are many out there ministering to incontinent and belligerent patients from whom a word of thanks will never be spoken. It takes great courage to do what many wouldn't do for a million dollars yet there are many doing it. They rank as prime exhibitors of what the Duke of Wellington tabbed as three o'clock in the morning courage.

Our first reading today records a portion from the prophet Isaiah where "the suffering servant" is in great prominence and it has the suffering servant mouthing the expression: "I will set my face like flint!" an expression alluding to that servant's willingness to endure the suffering that would be forthcoming in his life. That expression would later describe Christ's sentiments as he began his march to Calvary, a march which required cold-blooded courage, a march which required three-o'clock-in-the-morning courage.

That widow with the three children; that mother pushing her wheelchair-bound son; that sculptor with the one hand; that kid at that telescope; the fighter of lost causes; the gentle soul cleaning feces off that homeless man; it can be said of them that they "set their faces like flint." It can be said of them that they took on suffering few would have the moxie to endure. They exhibited what the Duke of Wellington would describe as three-o'clock-in-the-morning courage. That exhibition, their being like Christ, has resulted in much grace entering our world and, along with it, a lot of inspiration for the world to come.

Almost

Scripture Lesson: John 18: 33-37
"...Pilate said to Jesus: 'Are you the King of the Jews?'"

A word that's often attached to an unfulfilled life.

When I was in high school, I was asked to play the lead role in *A Man for All Seasons*. I had never acted before. I wasn't even a member of the drama club. After giving it some thought, I realized I couldn't pass on such a prestigious opportunity so I said yes and began in earnest to study my lines. The play was to be a major production, with girls from Mercy Academy being members of the cast. After three weeks of practicing and rehearsing our parts, word came that there would be no play. Bishop James McNulty, the local bishop at the time, learned that girls were being cast in a seminary play and that wasn't going to happen under his watch. The play was cancelled and my career as a stage performer came to a screeching halt. A potential future career on Broadway would be no more. I would forever be left to ponder how I was almost an actor in a leading role.

I reference that piece from my personal history because I'd like to talk with you today about that word "almost." It's one of the saddest words in any man or woman's dictionary. It ranks up there with "nearly," "next time," "if only" and "just about." Whenever the word gets spoken, you can bet on hearing descriptions of missed opportunities, aborted efforts, fumbled chances and lost dreams.

"I almost won the lottery."
"I almost made it to the Major Leagues."
"I almost won the contest."
"I almost bowled a perfect game."
"I almost made a hole in one."
"I almost broke the record."
"I almost played the lead role in *A Man for All Seasons*."

Now it's one thing when the "almost" is applied to games or plays or matters of relative unimportance, but it's another thing when the "almost" is applied to matters of great importance, matters relevant and significant when it comes to life. Take Pilate in today's Gospel! He almost performed what would have been history's greatest act of mercy. He almost pardoned the Prince of Peace. He almost released the Son of God. He almost opted to acquit Jesus Christ. He had the power. He had the choice. The option to free God's Son was his and …"He did it!"… Well, he almost did it.

That's the most tragic aspect of the word "almost." Those six ugly letters are often fixed onto epitaphs for lives that could have been, lives that could have been richer and greater and far more extraordinary, lives that could have registered a major impact on life. There have been many a Pilate who were almost heroes, almost a man or woman to be admired, almost a man or woman of Lincolnesque qualities, almost a significant player in the betterment of our human condition. But unfortunately for them and for us, they'll be forever remembered for the "almost" and not the "actual"; forever remembered for what could have been instead of for what was.

What I'd like for us to consider today are the promptings for the "almost"? What is it that keeps us from doing what we "almost" did? What is it that holds us back from achieving what we "almost" achieved? Well, first of all, we'll often do as Pilate did. We'll give in to voices other than our own, we'll give in to voices urging us to ignore our instincts, urging us to do or not do what we know in our heart of hearts we should do or not do.

One of my favorite stories involves a young boy walking onto a beach where he sees a very old man preparing to catch crabs. The young boy had never seen anyone catch crabs before so he sat in the sand and watched. The old crabber worked his strings and nets and soon began to catch one crab after another. Upon catching them, he'd throw the crabs into a huge bucket. It wasn't long before the little boy noticed crab legs inching over the top of the bucket. "Mister!" the young boy said to the old crabber, "You'd better put a lid on your bucket otherwise your crabs will get away."

"Not a chance," said the old crabber to the boy, "you see whenever one of them gets to the top, the other crabs will pull him down."

There are a lot of voices out there similar to the ones Pilate heard. Voices making us fearful of rising above the crowd, voices calling us down to a common level, voices discouraging us from standing up for what we know to be true and right. There are crabs galore in life and the more we listen to their voices the more likely it will be that an "almost" will be engraved upon our epitaphs.

So, first and foremost, the voices of crabs are what prompts us not to do what we almost did, not to achieve what we almost achieved. And so it goes as well for the voice of fear.

There is an old Sufi story about a man who's told that something terrible is going to happen to him. So he withdraws from life and begins to live a very protected existence, keeping away from people and doing his best to stay away from trouble. One day, while walking in the cemetery, he sees an old woman throwing herself on the grave of her husband. She's weeping and calling out his name. Witnessing her grief and witnessing the great love that lied behind it, he realizes that the terrible thing he would experience was that nothing like that would ever happen to him, that he'd never be privy to such a wonderful relationship, that he'd never experience a love that deep. The woman showed him a love that is the glory of life and that glory would never be his because of fear.

There's no question that the voice of fear is real and loud and it speaks of the hurt we may have to suffer or the pain we may have to endure or the bad things that may happen to us should we leave our protected existence, should we exit our comfort zone, should we venture into territory not charted on the maps of which we are familiar.

I was reading where centuries ago mapmakers would sketch a dragon on the edge of their maps indicating a territory as yet unexplored. The dragon served as a warning to explorers, a warning that if they entered that territory, they would be doing so at a great and tremendous risk. One set of explorers would heed the dragon warning and stay within the boundaries of the known world. There was another set of explorers, however, who did not heed the dragon warning. They boldly crossed over to where the other explorers had feared to tread. It was they who made it into our history books. The explorers who heeded the dragon warning never did. They were left to ponder how they "almost" discovered a new and exciting world.

The voice of fear is the voice of a dragon. We can allow it to doom us to an "almost" existence or we can ignore it and take on the risks and hurts and pain necessary to achieve the glory which, not unlike that man in the Sufi story, we may have otherwise never achieved.

And then there are the voices of doubt and despair. One of the fans of syndicated columnist Dear Abby once wrote to thank her for a letter she published that had changed her life. This fan wanted to return to school to become a teacher but was concerned because she would be 40 upon graduation. "Then," she said, "I read a letter in your column from someone in a similar situation and after reading your response, I decided to enroll in our local college." Along with that letter, Abby reprinted the original one. It was written by a 36-year-old college dropout who always wanted to be a doctor. He wrote to Abby because he was hesitating about returning to college and pursuing his dream because it would take seven years before he could ever function as a doctor and by then he'd be 43 years of age. He asked Abby what she thought. Abby responded with a simple question. She asked the writer as to how old he'd be in seven years if he didn't go to medical school.

There are many an almost physician, many an almost nurse, many an almost teacher, many an almost poet, many an almost nun, many an almost opera singer and they bear the "almost" moniker because they despaired that their age made their dream prohibitive, they despaired that they were too old to do what they wanted to do and, unfortunately for them, there was no Dear Abby to set them straight.

It's a shame as to how so many individuals have forsaken a desired vocation or have forsaken the nurturing of a real talent because they doubted that they were up to the task, they despaired that the circumstances of their life were such that it wasn't going to be possible for them to realize their dream.

I love the story of the 90-year-old who, when asked if she could play the piano, responded that she didn't know. And when she was further asked as to how it was that she didn't know, she had a great answer. She smiled and said: "I never tried!"

You have to wonder as to how many of those almost physicians or nurses or teachers or journalists or opera singers or whatever, you have to wonder as to how many of them could have shed the "almost" moniker had they at least tried to do what the voice of despair or doubt told them to be foolish or impossible to do.

And then finally when it comes to our not doing what we almost did or not achieving what we almost achieved, there is the matter of our listening to the voices of yesterday.

There was a play on Broadway many years ago that was entitled *The Echoing Mountain*. It was written by E.P. Templeton. Every character in the play at some time or another did something or said something of which he or she was ashamed. As the story unfolds, they each come to learn of the secret history of everyone of the characters. They each come to learn as to what it was the other had written or said or did that was the cause of their shame. So they each began to plot as to how they could use that information to their advantage. But the more they thought about it, the more they came to realize that it would only result in a multiplication of misery for themselves as well as for the others. They each came to see that in every life there are things that must not only be forgiven but they must also be forgotten. At the climax of the play, one hears in the background the vigorous slamming of many doors. It was an expressive symbol of their putting their past behind them and starting life anew.

That play drives home the point of how our yesterdays can weigh us down. How what we may have done in the past, even what we may have had done to us in the past, how it can only serve to hold us back from living. How it can only serve to hold us back from moving forward with life. All too often and on far too many occasions an "almost" has prefaced a life because the door wasn't slammed on yesterday, because something from the past prevented the move to a much more positive future.

"He or she almost got their act together."

"He or she almost got out of that rut."

"He or she almost ended that feud."

"He or she almost became a breath of fresh air, almost bounced back, and almost made us proud." But unfortunately they listened too intently to the voices of yesterday.

So, my friends, do not become someone whose claim to fame is an "almost." Do not follow the lead of Pilate in our Gospel. Slam the door on yesterday! Resist the pull of the crabs! Don't fear the dragon! Pay heed to Abby's wisdom! Do that and there will be no "almost" engraved upon your epitaphs. Do that and not only will you be pleased, but God will be pleased as well.

Yes

Scripture Lesson: II Corinthians 1:18-22
"...Jesus Christ was not alternately 'yes' and 'no,' he was never anything but 'yes'..."

Responding in the affirmative can make for a rich and extraordinary life.

There was a promising young businessman who had a serious flaw. He found it difficult to give a clear yes or no answer to anything. The flaw became a matter of great concern to company officials, prompting them to contact a psychiatrist to work with him on the problem. Upon greeting the young businessman, the psychiatrist said: "I understand you are having trouble making decisions?" The young man looked at the psychiatrist and said: "Well, yes and no!"

We heard in today's second reading that the Son of God, unlike that young businessman, was not alternately "yes" and "no," he was never anything but "yes." And that being so, we, his followers, are called to be the same and our faithfulness to that call can make all the difference in the world when it comes to our character, our integrity and our esteem. Our willingness to say "yes" can positively effect the quality of life of those with whom we work, with whom we play and with whom we live.

Let us first consider the willingness to say: "Yes I am!" I'm not sure if many of you are familiar with CPE but it is an acronym for

Clinical Pastoral Education. In essence, it's a program designed for those aspiring to the ministry, be they Catholic, Protestant, Jewish etc. One of the components of that program is something called a verbatim, which is the recapturing of a conversation one might have had with a hospital patient or member of a parish. Whenever one shares that verbatim with the others involved in the program, those others are free to ask any questions relative to the conversation, questions that can be very personal, very challenging and sometimes frightening. They are often questions inquiring as to how one was feeling or what was going through their mind in the course of the verbal exchange sketched in the verbatim. In a majority of the cases, the verbatim presenter neither wants to nor is ready to answer such questions because their doing so would involve the revelation of fears, imperfections, or inner pains they'd just as soon keep secret. What they fail to realize is that unless they are willing to be truthful as to their feelings, unless they are willing to admit to their flaws and shortcomings, they're not going to be effective ministers, priests, or chaplains, because they'll be lacking the honesty and authenticity which those professions require.

And what holds true for verbatim presenters holds true for us. Far too many of us choose to wear masks, we put on these facades that hide from others our real and true selves leaving them to wonder if we really meant what we happened to say, leaving them to wonder if we are the person we had claimed to be.

Being courageous and willing to say: "Yes, I am not perfect! Yes, I am lonely! Yes, I am afraid! Yes, I am inadequate!" Being courageous and willing to say as "Popeye" would say: "I am what I am and that's all that I am!" That demands honesty; that requires openness, that necessitates a willingness to be authentic. But when such a "yes" is spoken, it makes for an individual easier to get along with, and live with, and love.

Right beside the statement "Yes I am!" sits the statement "Yes I did!" You may have occasionally come across the cartoon in the daily newspaper called the Family Circus. The cartoon often depicts an invisible figure usually appearing in the background or in the corner of the frame whenever the mother or father asks the children as to whether or not they had done something wrong. They might ask if they left their father's tools in the yard or if they put their fingerprints on the wall. The typical response is: "Not me!" and the invisible figure in the corner of the cartoon depicts this character called "Not me." Well, many a person follows the lead of those children; many a person passes the blame for their wrongdoing onto the figure called "not me." They do not take responsibility for a mistake they may have made or a sin they may have committed.

I like that story I heard recently about a scuffle in an elementary school playground. The teacher in charge finally restores order and then says in a loud voice: "How did all this get started?" One of the kids points to another and says: "It all started when he hit me back!"

Being willing and courageous enough to say "Yes I did" when asked about having done what we knew to be wrong, being willing and courageous enough to say "Yes I did" when it comes to assuming rightful blame for a mistake that had been made; that speaks of accountability, that speaks of responsibility! We're seen as someone who can be trusted and counted on to own up to what most others would excuse away.

And alongside "Yes, I am!" and "Yes, I did!" there rests the statement "Yes, I care!" I am reminded of Bill Sands who was listed as an incorrigible prisoner. He was locked in solitary confinement facing many years in prison. His father was dead and his mother refused to answer any of his letters and he didn't feel as though there was a soul around who cared or even realized that he was alive. So one day while he was sitting in his 9 x 6 cell, the warden, Clinton Duffy, happened to come by. He says to him: "Why don't you try to prepare yourself for life outside of prison?" Bill looked at him and smiled and said: "Why should I, nobody cares about me, absolutely nobody." The warden looks him in the eyes and compassionately and tenderly says: "I care!"

That statement proved to be the beginning of a miracle for it led to the transformation of the life of Bill Sands. He would not only soon leave the prison but he went on to found the Severin Foundation which has helped countless numbers of ex-convicts begin a new life.

There are people all over the world today who feel very much as did Bill Sands in that jail cell, people whose eyes telegraph the message: "No one cares about me!" The more who step forward as did that warden, the more who step forward and say: "Yes I care about you!" the more will be the positive transformations of people who would otherwise die broken, forgotten and lost. Being courageous enough to say "Yes, I care!" speaks of compassion, it speaks of empathy, it speaks of kindness, all of which can make us shining lights in a world darkened by apathy and callousness and hate.

Being a "Yes" person as Jesus was a "Yes" person makes us a standout amongst our peers because, first of all, we're authentic, there's no mask hiding whom we are; second, we're accountable, we're unafraid to assume responsibility; third, we're compassionate, ready and willing to show we care; and fourth, we're confident and positive. When others say: "No I can't!" we say instead: "Yes I can!"

One of the finest sports writers in America was a man by the name of Herb Fullerton. He once told the story of a manager of a San Antonio baseball team. His team was supposed to have been the finest team in the league but the team had lost 17 of their first 20 games. It just so happened there was a revival meeting going on near the ballpark and this meeting was being conducted by a faith healing evangelist who was attracting a lot of attention because of the miracles he could allegedly perform. Word was that it would take a miracle to turn the team around. A light went on in the head of the manager. He told each of the members of his team to give him their two favorite bats. He loaded them into a wheel barrel and asked that they stay put till he got back. In two hours, he jubilantly returns telling the players that he had taken the bats to the revival meeting and had the faith healing evangelist bless each and every bat. "There's a special power now within them!' so said the manager. The next day San Antonio played Dallas and San Antonio got 37 hits and scored 20 runs and from that day forward they were the team to beat. They went on and won the pennant and ultimately the Championship.

When asked about the blessing of those bats, the manager admitted that it was all a ruse. He never did take them to the revival meeting.

The players, however, didn't know that and they stepped to the plate believing their bat held special powers, convinced that their bat could and would deliver hits. And deliver them they did and it was the team's hitting prowess which led to the turnaround of the season.

If we approach anything with a positive attitude, if we say firmly and resolutely: "Yes, I can!" when there's some question as to our ability to meet a challenge, you'd be surprised as to the difference it will make in accomplishing what the challenge had required us to do. As that San Antonio baseball team had shown, confidence and a positive attitude can work miracles; it can be the deciding factor when it comes to victory or defeat. Being willing and courageous enough to say: "Yes, I can!" speaks of an upbeat and positive spirit that makes for winning not only in baseball but in life as well.

So being a "Yes!" person means: "Yes, I can! Yes, I did! Yes, I care! Yes, I am! and also Yes, I will!" There was a mother who found herself doing most of the household chores. One evening, she's off to a meeting and her husband and teenage son decide it would be good if they cleaned up the kitchen and so they did. They wrapped up the leftovers, washed all the pots and pans, cleaned all the dishes, put everything away. They even mopped the floor. Feeling good about the job they did, they eagerly awaited Mom's return. Two hours later, she walks in, takes off her coat, hangs it up, and walks right through the sparkling clean kitchen and into the den where she sits down to read the newspaper. Dumbfounded that she didn't say a word about the clean kitchen, the father goes into the den and stammers: "We cleaned up the kitchen! Didn't you notice?" His wife replied: "Yes I noticed!" Then she paused and said: "Thankless job, isn't it?"

Thankless jobs are plentiful in the world in which we live and there are very few takers. There are all kinds of messy, dirty tasks begging for volunteers to do them, all kinds of ugly chores yearning for someone to take them on. Those who hear that summons to help and courageously steps forward and says: "Yes I will!" are amongst the most admirable and the most praiseworthy of people. In taking on the work no one wants to do, he or she stands out as a model of unselfishness, a symbol of generosity and a portrait of sacrifice.

And then, finally, when it comes to being a "Yes!" person, there's the willingness to say: "Yes I do!" Evangelist Billy Graham reported that, during a visit to the campus of Harvard University several years back, he asked Harvard President Dr. Bok as to what in his opinion was most lacking in the mindset of students of today. Dr. Bok replied: "a sense of commitment."

I'm reminded of the young man who walked into a card shop looking for the appropriate card for his girlfriend, a card where he could express to her his undying love. The sales clerk showed him one that read: "To the only girl I ever loved!"

"That's great!" said the young man. "I'll take six of them!"

These days and times in which we live seem to find fewer and fewer who are willing to commit to a cause or to commit to a vocation or willing, for that matter, to commit to someone they love. Being willing and courageous enough to say: "Yes, I do!" speaks of dedication and it speaks of a willingness to assume the risks and sacrifices necessary to see to the end that which we had vowed to do.

Saying: "Yes, I am! will speak to our authenticity. Saying "Yes, I did!" will speak to our responsibility and accountability. Saying "Yes, I care!" will speak to our compassion. Saying "Yes, I can!" will speak to our positive spirit. Saying "Yes, I will!" will speak to our generosity. Saying "Yes, I do!" will speak to our commitment. Following the lead of Jesus and being a "yes" person will make for a rich, beautiful, and extraordinary life.

A Troubling Friendship

Scripture Lesson: Luke 12: 49-53
"…Do you think I've come to establish peace on earth? No, I tell you…"

Being a friend of God spells trouble.

One of the more humorous anecdotes from The Lives of the Saints is the one where St. Teresa of Avila is complaining to God about all the troubles God seemed to be sending into her life. God said to her: "Teresa that's the way I treat all of my friends." To which this spunky Saint replied: "Then no wonder that you have so few."

Now, I'm not one to believe that God sends us trouble but I am one to believe that it isn't all that easy being a friend of God. I am one to believe that if we strike up a relationship with the Almighty, troubles will invariably follow. There's first of all the trouble of change.

I always liked that story about a woman who came home from the gift shop with a beautiful plaque. It read "Prayer Changes Things." She put it over the fireplace in the den and it looked great. A short time later, the woman went to the grocery store and, when she returned, the plaque was missing. "What happened to my plaque?" she asked her husband. "I took it down!" he replied. "Took it down?" she said. "Why? Don't you believe in prayer?" The husband replied: "Of course I believe in prayer. It's change I can't stand."

We can chuckle at that husband's reply but I'm not so sure we can chuckle at the husband's sentiments. Change is not something we tolerate too well nor is it something we readily embrace for invariably it involves disruptions to our life. When it comes to being a friend of God, disruptions and change are to be expected.

Take Zaccheus. He was a tax collector who was apparently fairly content with his life until he became a friend of Jesus. Not long thereafter, it became clear that he needed to change and radically so. He needed to be more honest in his tax collecting. He needed to make amends for his years of embezzling. He needed to overhaul his attitude and priorities. All of which had to be a very troubling and a very distressing thing to do.

Or take the rich young man. He was quite complacent, quite content and pretty happy with himself, that is, till he tried to be friend of Jesus. He figured that Jesus would be impressed that he was following all the commandments and when he met Jesus, he was horrified to discover that Jesus was unimpressed and furthermore he found that if he wanted a relationship with Jesus he would have to sell all of his earthly goods. That proved to be too troubling a thing to do and the scriptures record that he went away sad.

To be a friend of God, to be a friend of Jesus requires life style changes. It requires that the business of our life not be conducted in its usual way. There are favorite sins we need to stop committing. There are broken relationships that we need to mend. There's time for prayer we need to find. There is the cynicism and surliness that we need to end. Friendship with God requires many changes and change is quite the troublesome thing to do.

And then there's the matter of service. Being a friend of God requires a commitment to service. There's a famous World War II story about a statue of Jesus in a bombed out church. The statute portrayed Jesus as reaching out to the world and, in the devastation of the bombing, the hands of the statute were broken off. For a long time thereafter, the statue without hands stood as it was found and upon the outstretched arms someone hung a sign. The sign read: "He has no hands but yours."

I'm reminded of the story of a man who stood before God, complaining about all the anguish and distress in the world and why it was that God didn't send help. "I did send help!" God replied. "I sent you."

Being a friend of God means that we're expected to step in for him wherever and whenever there are people hurting. We're expected to be his hands when work is needed in some corner of life where some tragedy or disaster may have taken place. Being a friend of God means we can't sit idly by when there's someone in pain or anguish. It means we can't rest content when there's a child hungry, a widow that's lonely, or a man or woman on the streets with no place to call a home. Being a friend of God means that we're going to be constantly called upon to be of service to those in need and so our lives are going to be disrupted on a regular basis and that's a troubling thought for any of us to ponder.

Then there's the matter of evangelization. There is a made up story that describes Jesus' return to heaven after his life had ended. The angels gathered around him to find out about all the things that happened while he was gone. Jesus explained to the angels how he shared his teachings, expressed his love, died on the cross and then was resurrected so he might declare to the entire world that a new Kingdom was now at hand. When Jesus finished telling the story, Michael the Archangel asked the Lord: "What happens now?"

Jesus answered: "I left behind a handful of faithful men and women. They will tell the story. They will express the love. They will spread the kingdom."

"But what if they fail?" asked Michael. "What will be the plan then?"

Jesus answered Michael by saying: "There is no other plan."

Being a friend of God means that it is our responsibility to evangelize. It's our responsibility to tell the world the good news of the Lord Jesus Christ. It's our responsibility to let others in on the truth of God's love. There really is no one else to do it. There really is no other plan. So friendship with God provides us with the troubling thought that the salvation of many a soul rests in our hands, the troubling thought that someone might go to their grave impoverished and lost and broken because they hadn't heard from us about the saving love of God.

Then there's the matter of accountability. An old Hasidic tale tells of the Rabbi who hired a coachman and carriage to take him and others to a neighboring village. The carriage was making its way along a road with fruit trees and orchards on either side. At one point, the coachman stopped by the road and told his passengers: "I'm going to climb over the fence and steal some of that fruit. You stay here and keep an eye out for anyone coming. Let me know if anyone sees me." He had just crossed the fence when the Rabbi called out: "Someone's watching!" The driver quickly jumped back over the fence and into the wagon and drove a bit further and stopped. He told the passengers: "I am going to try again. Make sure I'm not being seen." Once again as soon as he crossed the fence, the Rabbi called out: "Someone's watching!" The driver now was furious. He said: "I don't understand it. The road is empty, the area is deserted, and I don't see another human being for miles. Yet every time I tried to grab some fruit, you tell me: "Someone's watching! What's going on?" The Rabbi pointed heavenward and simply said: "Someone is watching!"

Once we've established a friendship with God, there's no getting away from God and that spells the troubling thought that there is nothing we do that is devoid of God's attention, there's no action we can perform that won't be answerable to God. So try as we may to sneak one past the Almighty, it cannot happen because someone's watching all the time and that someone is God, our friend.

And then, there's the matter of conscience. In the village of Shelburne, England a visitor in town may be shown this famous row of trees, which the famed author Gordon White planted around his parsonage. They were planted by White to shut out the view of the cattle slaughterhouses that happened to surround the area where the parsonage stood. That's often something we do when we see things not to our liking. When we see ugliness, injustice, prejudice or bigotry, we tend to look for a way to block them from our conscience. If we call ourselves a friend of God, we can't do that. We can't put up trees to block the slaughterhouses of life. We must speak out. We must voice a protest. We must work to put an end to the cruelties and the injustices and the ugliness around us.

The problem is that our doing so will not be taken kindly. Many of those injustices and cruelties have been going on a long time and there are many benefitting from their maintenance. Unpopularity, condemnation, ridicule and hostility will invariably follow any sort of protest on our part for it's sure to upset the many who have a vested interest in what it is we happen to be protesting. Being a friend of God means having a heightened conscience and that will demand our noticing and condemning sins which had previously eluded our attention.

And finally, there is the matter of excellence. On Wednesday evening during his presidency, Abraham Lincoln would go to hear the preacher at the New York Avenue Presbyterian Church right near the White House. Lincoln was leaving the service one night when one of his assistants asked him what he thought of the sermon. "Well," said Lincoln, "the content was excellent and the preacher spoke with great eloquence but it lacked one essential quality."

"What might that be?" asked the assistant. Lincoln responded: "The preacher forgot to ask us to do something great."

One of the troubling aspects of being a friend of God is that God expects us to do something great. And that means no slouching, no half-hearted efforts, no giving of a fraction of our powers. Gustav Mahler put it best when he said: "we are to be as beautiful as we can be in every way for ugliness," and I'll add mediocrity, "is an insult to a beautiful God." So our being a friend of God brings with it the news that mediocrity will no longer be tolerated. We need to go to the trouble of always giving our all to whatever we plan to do.

Jesus in our Gospel tells us that he didn't come to establish peace but came instead to establish trouble and, when you think of it, that's precisely what we're facing should we establish ties with him and the Gospel. Those ties will demand change and unlike prayer, it's something most of us can't stand. It will also demand service. It's expected that we be God's hands. It will demand evangelization and the troubling truth that there is no backup plan if we fail. It will demand accountability which means we can't go anywhere without God watching our every move. Our tie to Jesus and the Gospels will make for a heightened conscience which will mean getting grief for protesting those slaughterhouses we had previously pretended not to see. It will demand from us excellence which means going to the trouble of giving everything our best. Friendship with Jesus, friendship with God is indeed a daunting task.

When you come right down to it, St. Teresa of Avila had every right in the world to complain of the trouble God brings into the life of his friends. Perhaps that really is why so few of us can truly lay a claim to that friendship.

Saying Thank You

Scripture Lesson: Luke 17: 11-19
"…Has none but this foreigner returned to give thanks to God?"

The saying of "thank you" can reap rich and powerful blessings.

The credit-card division of Citibank has embarked upon an advertising campaign which attempts to highlight the rewards the bank will provide to those who use their card. The campaign revolves around the words "thank you." In one humorous commercial, a couple is sitting in a restaurant and the man is asked point-blank as to his intentions as far as their relationships is concerned. She is tired of their courtship and she wants a definite answer: "Is he going to marry her or not?" The man squirms and stutters and stammers and then suddenly blurts out the words "thank you." His mate is so struck by those words that his answer to her question no longer matters. She gushes in appreciation over the loveliness of that thank you.

In another commercial, one shopper in a grocery store innocently inquires about another shopper's pregnancy only to be angrily grilled as to the reason for the inquiry, seeing how she wasn't pregnant at all. Like the man at that restaurant, she squirms and stutters and stammers and then blurts out the words "thank you" and the other shopper is so struck by those words that her anger melts into joy and she gushes in appreciation for that thank you that she heard.

Now it would be nice if life worked the same way. It would be nice if the words "thank you" could work the magic they worked in those commercials. But even though they can't, that's not to say that they couldn't work other magic. That's not to say that the utterance of thank you couldn't be a source of a rich and bountiful blessing.

Take the matter of healing. Dr. A. J. Cronin, the famed British writer, told of a physician of his acquaintance who prescribed a thank-you cure for discouraged and defeated patients. Whenever such a patient would present himself or herself to that physician and the doctor could find no physical reason for the problem, he would prescribe that the patient say thank you for six weeks when anyone did him or her a favor. And, according to A. J. Cronin, the physician had a good cure rate.

Dr. Norman Vincent Peale writes of a Bill Stidger who had hit the depths of despondency and despair. For his cure, he was told to write a letter of thanks to the various people in his past who had been of great benefit to him. He remembered an old school teacher. He remembered her as a great source of inspiration. He remembered how she had given him an appreciation of literature. So he wrote a letter of thanks for the gift she'd been to him. A week later, she wrote back. She told him that his was the first letter of thanks she had ever received. She told him she would cherish his letter to the day she died. That response brought a huge smile to Stidger's face and a ray of sunshine to his mind and it encouraged him to write other letters of thanks to other people who were helpful to him. Five hundred letters were written in all. Not only did the writing lift him from his despondency and despair, but so did the responses. And in the years that followed, whenever depression or despair would rear its ugly head, he'd go back to those letters of thanks and their responses and the happiness he experienced in that enterprise would well up inside his heart once again.

One could well say that there's much to be said for the healing properties of gratitude, much to be said for the ability of a thank you to lift a person up from the doldrums of depression and despair.

And besides its ability to heal, it's also been shown that the saying of thank you can foster good mental health. There's an old legend that tells of a man who came one day to the barn where Satan stores the seeds he scatters across the earth. The man noticed that the two most abundant seeds in the barn were seeds of bitterness and discouragement. Satan told him that they were without question his most effective seeds. "Why those seeds will grow almost anywhere!" he said. But then a solemn look came upon Satan's face. "There's one place, however," said Satan, "where the seeds of bitterness and discouragement will not grow!" "Where might that be?" asked the man. And Satan answered: "They will not grow in a heart of gratitude."

Although it is a matter of legend, there's much to be said for its truth. The ability to say thank-you even in the midst of the worst of life situations has been known to hold off feelings of discouragement and bitterness.

I read of a 70-year-old man who called his son in panic because that morning he found his basement flooded. "Son," he said, "the bed, the rug, the couch, the TV, everything is under water. Everything is ruined!" The son paused for a moment and then said something that shocked his father. He said, "Gee, dad, that's great!" The father couldn't believe what he heard. "What's great?" he asked. "Well, Dad, what's great is that you woke up this morning!" The father paused and laughed and said, "Gee, son, I never considered that. I guess you're right." That man's son alerted his dad to something that warranted a thank you and that helped his dad from getting overly upset and discouraged by the flooding of his basement.

I'm reminded here of a man who practiced saying thank you in all circumstances. One day while driving to work he had a flat tire and had to pull onto the shoulder of the highway. Getting out of his car, he looked and prayed: "Thank you God for all of your gifts. Thank you that out of this world's six billion people, I belong to a small minority that has a car. Thank you for the wide shoulder on this highway that allows me to safely change the tire. Thank you that it's good weather, that it's not raining or snowing. Thank you that I have the physical ability to change a tire. Thank you God for these gifts on this day and for all of your gifts, Amen!"

I'm reminded of a prayer written by Matthew Henry, the old biblical scholar, after he got mugged and had his wallet stolen. The prayer read: "Lord, I am thankful first because I was never robbed before. Second, I am thankful that although they took my wallet, they did not take my life. Third, I'm thankful that it was I who was robbed and not I who was robbing."

Our learning to say thank you for the positive things that are still in place despite the negative happenings, our learning to say thank you that there are good things that have occurred even though bad things are going on around us, that sort of thankfulness can keep the devil from planting those seeds of bitterness and discouragement. That can keep our spiritual and mental health intact even though our lives have taken a negative turn.

And then there's the prestige which the saying of thank you can bestow. Theodore Roosevelt was an esteemed president in his day. What won him over in the hearts and souls of many was his gratefulness. On his whistlestop tours during his campaign trips, Roosevelt always made it a point to leave his private car to extend thanks to the engineer, the firemen, the clerks, and the kitchen aides, anyone on that train that helped assure a safe and comfortable ride. That was true of the White House staff and true as well for the staff of the hotels where he stayed and the auditoriums he would frequent. Theodore Roosevelt was referred to as a class act and that reference came in no small measure to the thank you's that so readily rolled off his tongue.

Our saying of thank you could well put us in the company of a Theodore Roosevelt. Our saying of thank you could well identify us as a class act, someone that's considerate and appreciative and humble. There's a lot of prestige that's gained in the utterance of a thank you.

And finally, our saying of thank you can fill us with great joy. There is an old Aesop fable that featured a lion, a fox and a donkey. They became partners and successfully acquired a large amount of food.

The lion asked the donkey to divide the food. Carefully, the donkey divided the spoils into three equal piles. The lion was offended, burst into a rage, and devoured the donkey. Then the lion asked the fox to make the division. The fox accumulated all they had killed into one large pile and left but a morsel for himself. The lion said: "That is perfect! Who taught you how to divide so well?" The fox replied: "I just recently learned it from the donkey."

There are a lot of things we've learned from previous generations that have spared us heavy pain. There are a lot people who have suffered and died for things, which now we know to avoid thanks to their having suffered and died. There's much we've learned from noble and brave souls that have spared us the work of learning about them ourselves.

The famed Australian preacher F.W. Boreham, whom I so often like to quote, wrote once of our giving thanks to the someone who discovered that horseradish lends zest to roast beef; the someone who discovered that applesauce goes well with pork chops; the someone who found that red currant jelly enhances the flavor of venison and mint jelly enhances the flavor of lamb chops; the someone who found that strawberries taste better with whipped cream. Boreham wrote as to how numerous nauseous combinations had to have been tried and tasted before these appetizing combinations were launched upon the world and how lucky and blessed we are that we didn't have to engage in those culinary experiments.

If in our saying of thank you, we call to mind the people who suffered and died so we might learn a lesson we're lucky to have learned; if in our saying of thank you, we call to mind those who did the spade work for the delicacies of life we enjoy; happiness will fill our hearts for we'll come to realize how we've been richly and wonderfully blessed.

In our Gospel today, Jesus healed ten lepers and only one came to give thanks and it bothered Jesus that the other nine appeared to be ungrateful. The Gospel serves as a call for all of us to be grateful, for all of us to make it a point to say thank you more often. By doing so, by saying thank you more often, we will reap bountiful blessings.

There's the healing it can bring to the despondency we may feel. There is the ability to ward off Satan's planting of those seeds of bitterness and discouragement. There's its identification of us as a class act and there is the joy that will fill our hearts as we realize how lucky we are. Our saying thank you may not work the magic they worked in those Citibank credit-card commercials, but they will work magic and we'll be the beneficiaries of that magic.

The Devil's Favorite Tool

Scripture Lesson: Luke 3: 1-6
"...Every valley shall be filled and every mountain and hill shall be made low..."

Some thoughts to consider should we be tempted by despair.

An old Mexican tale tells of the day the devil decided to go out of business. He sent word throughout the land that an auction would be held for the tools he used to lead people astray. As expected, crowds gathered from all around who were able and willing to pay great sums of money to secure one of those tools. When the moment arrived for the sale to begin, the room buzzed with excitement. One by one items were brought forward to be auctioned but to everyone's surprise they looked shiny and new as if they had never been used and, as a result, they received few if any bids. Finally the moment arrived that everyone had been waiting for as onto the stage came an old and worn device. Everyone took notice. No one appeared to recognize what it was but most felt sure that it must be something special and powerful. While the crowd talked among themselves, a potential buyer got inside information that the device was Satan's favorite tool. One of the devil's assistants explained: "It's what you humans called despair," he said. "Satan found that once you can get someone to give up hope and embrace despair, you could pretty much do with them anything that you want."

There's much truth to that Mexican tale. Despair can cripple a life, immobilize a life, and destroy a life like nothing else can. So what I'd like to share with you are some thoughts to consider should despair enter your life, should you, in fact, be tempted by the Devil's favorite tool. First, you might consider the fact that what might appear as hopeless may just need a little more time.

In 1939, the MGM studio released a movie which it thought would be a box office smash. The movie was entitled *The Wizard of Oz*. I don't know how many of you are aware of the fact that initially it was no hit at all. It was a box office flop. Critics panned it, with one of them writing that the movie displayed no imagination and lacked what it took for greatness. MGM buried the movie in one of its warehouse vaults. Eighteen years later, someone came across the movie and decided to show it on a new medium called television. The rest, as they say, is history. *The Wizard of Oz* became a huge hit and won the acclaim of millions. It ranks as one of the top-selling videos of all time. It could well be said that *The Wizard of Oz* needed 18 years to be appreciated for its greatness, 18 years to achieve its hoped for glory.

A similar story can be had for Herman Melville's *Moby Dick*, the classic story of the big white whale. When first published, it hardly sold as many a critic considered it a worthless piece of trash. It would take 70 years for that book and for Herman Melville to be recognized for their greatness.

Should the devil tempt us with despair, we need but think of *Moby Dick* and *The Wizard of Oz*. It might well be that what we're despairing about may need a bit more time. What we had thought would be successful, what we had thought would work out, may in fact be so and do so but it will take our hanging on to hope a little while longer.

The next thing to consider should the devil tempt us with his favorite tool is that no matter how hopeless things may seem, all may not be lost. I always liked that story about a psychologist and his two sons, one being an incurable pessimist and the other being an incurable optimist. One Christmas he decided to try and cure the both of them of their maladies. While they slept on Christmas Eve, he crept into the pessimist's room and filled it with immense amounts of toys and then crept into the optimist's room and filled that room with a load of horse manure. Christmas morning came and he went to the pessimist's room and there his son was sitting, not very happy at all looking, in fact, very down. "Son," said the Dad, "Don't you know all those toys are for you?"

"Yes, I know that," said the boy, "but I'm afraid that if I move I'll break them." The father then went to the optimist's room and that son was smiling and laughing and singing and throwing the horse manure in the air. The Dad said to him: "Son, don't you know that what you're tossing in the air is horse manure?"

"Sure, I know it, Dad," said the boy, "but the way I figure it, with all this horse poop there's got to be a pony!"

Now, I'm not trying to tell you that you'll find a pony in the horse poop that's triggering your despair, but I am trying to tell you that all may not be lost, that there may be some good that will be found even though what you hoped for will never come to pass. It might be that a lesson will be learned or an insight gained or a positive change prompted which will, in fact, improve and better your life, that will more than make up for the disappointment and dejection which you might happen to be feeling. So should despair seem awfully tempting, we needn't succumb to its lure. Although our hopes have been dashed, all has not been lost. With all of that manure, there may well be a pony.

The third thing to consider should the devil tempt us with his favorite tool is the real and distinct possibility that something unexpected and unanticipated will occur that will change the entire picture. I refer here to that oft-told story of the two frogs that fell into a can of cream. They thrashed around desperately trying to hop out but they were unable to do so. One frog decided to give up. "It's hopeless!" he said, and following one last try to hop out, he gave up and sank to the bottom of the can where he drowned. The other frog refused to give up. He was bound and determined to keep on trying and, with all that thrashing, the cream began to turn to butter and the frog stepped on a lump of the butter and jumped out to safety and to freedom.

I realize that I just related a fairy tale but the fact of the matter is that unexpected things do happen, unforeseen developments do occur, and out of the blue incidents always lie within the realm of possibility. So it might well be that when things look hopeless and bleak, something that no one had thought of or anticipated as being capable of happening does in fact happen thus changing the entire course of events.

I attended a medical ethics conference not too long ago and one of the cases being reviewed was that of a child about to be born whose kidneys functioned so poorly that it was anticipated the child would have to undergo dialysis immediately upon birth and chances were that the child would be tethered to a dialysis machine the rest of his life. In doing a burden vs. benefit analysis of that case, someone pointed out that the burden of dialysis could change dramatically over the next 10 to 20 years. That it could well be that when the child reaches 20, medical or technological advancements may be such that what may appear burdensome today will not be so tomorrow.

And beside the unexpected trumping our despair, there's also the possibility that advancements or breakthroughs in technology or science will soon come to pass that will cast a whole different light on what we may be despairing about.

Then there's the long and distinguished list of individuals who have proven that what may appear to be hopeless may in fact not be hopeless at all. Consider Fyodor Dostoevsky who survived four years in a Siberian prison camp and fought a debilitating illness and whom everyone had written off as ever being able do anything with his life. He went on to become one of the world's greatest novelists. Or take Helen Keller, blind and deaf at 19 months of age yet went on to graduate from Radcliff College with honors and went on to become a renowned lecturer and celebrated author. History is filled with a long distinguished list of people who should have succumbed to despair but went on to do and accomplish what was termed hopeless and impossible for them to do or accomplish. So if the devil is trying to tempt you with despair, resist the temptation because, to borrow a phrase from the New York State Lottery: "Hey, you never know!"

Resist the temptation to despair, as well, because the good you do is never wasted. I point here to a definition of hope as given by the great Czechoslovakian President Vaclav Havel. He described hope as not the conviction that something will turn out well but the conviction that something makes sense regardless of how it turns out.

When author Lloyd Douglas attended college, he lived in a boardinghouse. It so happened that a retired wheelchair-bound music professor resided on the first floor. Each day Douglas would drop in on the professor for some words of wisdom. One morning he happened to come by and he asked the professor as to what the good news was that day. The professor took a tuning fork and tapped it on the side of his wheelchair. It made a sound that kept on going. "That sound," he said, "is what we refer to in the music world as middle C. It was middle C yesterday. It will be middle C tomorrow. It will be middle C a thousand years from now. The tenor upstairs sings flat. The soprano next door warbles off key. The piano across the hall is out of tune. But the good news, my friend, is that the sound of the tuning fork is always middle C."

The good we've done, the extra mile we've walked, the positive efforts we made, the honesty we had shown, the care we had given, the commitment that we kept, the trouble we had taken; it may not have resulted in any sort of blessing, it may not have resulted in our lives turning out for the better, it may not have resulted in any benefit of any kind. But we need not despair for we can take heart in the fact that it made sense regardless of the poor showing. It was middle C yesterday. It will be middle C tomorrow. It will be middle C a thousand years from now. Its light will forever shine despite the darkness tempting us to despair.

And then finally when it comes to things to consider should the devil tempt us with his favorite tool is the fact of the reality of God's presence despite the hopelessness that looms about. That's what got Corrie Ten Boom and her Dutch family through their bout with despair. They were a Christian family who tried to help the Jewish people escape the Nazi soldiers bent on their capture. One day they got caught and, as punishment, they were sent to the very same concentration camp as were the Jews. While there, their faith got severely tested. The temptation to despair was fierce. What kept them going was their belief, and this is Corrie Ten Boom's most famous quote, their belief that "there is no pit so deep that God is not deeper still!" God was with them in their fear and trepidation; God was present despite the bleak surroundings.

And so is that the case for each and every one of us. Though the pit we may be in is inviting us to despair, we needn't accept the invitation. God is at our side and God will see us through. God is our hope and our salvation.

We're into the second week of the Advent season, a season brimming with hope. Our Gospel today speaks of valleys being raised and mountains being laid low, a promise of hopeful times yet to come. Hope is what we're called to uphold and to cherish during these Advent days.

Should we find it difficult to hold on to hope, should the devil tempt us with his favorite tool, we need to keep in mind the movie *Wizard of Oz* and the novel *Moby Dick*. What may seem hopeless to succeed may just need a little more time. Should we find it difficult to hold on to hope, should the devil tempt us with despair, we need remember that all may not be lost. With all that manure, there may well be a pony. Should we find it difficult to hold on to hope, should the devil tempt us with despair, we need remember: "Hey, you never know!" The cream may turn to butter.

Should we find it difficult to hold on to hope, should the devil tempt us with despair, we need remember that the good we do is never wasted. It's middle C today. It will be middle C tomorrow. It will be middle C a thousand years from now. Should we find it difficult to hold on to hope, should the devil tempt us with despair, we need to remember that God is with us. God is our hope and our salvation. "There is no pit so deep that God is not deeper still."

Five Minutes Longer

Scripture Lesson: Luke 18: 1-8
"...Because the widow keeps bothering me, I shall deliver a just decision for her..."

Persistence and perseverance can make a difference.

Arthur Wellesley, the Duke of Wellington, has a special niche in history because he was the commander of the British soldiers who ultimately defeated Napoleon at the famous Battle of Waterloo. When Wellesley was asked as to what made that victory possible, he provided an interesting answer. He didn't lay claim to England's excellent strategy. He didn't say anything about mistakes Napoleon might have made. He didn't even point to the supremacy of the British soldier. He said, in fact, that the British soldiers were no braver than the French soldiers. According to Wellesley, what turned the tide, what proved to be the key to victory in the Battle of Waterloo was the fact that his soldiers could be brave for five minutes longer. It was the five minutes longer that made all the difference in the world.

It's the five minutes longer that I'd like to talk with you about today. It's persistence and perseverance I'd like to discuss with you today. Just as it was the difference maker in the Battle of Waterloo, so can it be the difference maker when it comes to the positive living of one's life.

Take the matter of greatness. I recently read an essay by F. W. Boreham[9] where he stipulated that the world's most distinguished individuals could be divided into three classes. There are those who, like the inventor, do extraordinary things. There are those who, like the poet or composer, do quite ordinary things in an extraordinary way. And then there are those who do quite ordinary things in a quite ordinary way but, because of their perseverance and persistence, they do those things on a quite extraordinary scale.

Take Christopher Columbus as an example. In all actuality, all he did was sail a ship. That was all. Many a mariner had done the same. What distinguished Columbus was that he held on to his westward course far more obstinately and far more persistently and far more perseveringly then had anybody else. One could say that, unlike the mariners before him, Columbus stayed the course five minutes longer.

We find a similar example in David Livingston. All he did was walk the soils of Africa. Many others had done the same before him. What distinguished Livingston was that he kept on walking. He kept on walking even though the muscles of his legs ached from sheer exhaustion. He kept on walking even after his body had become what he described as a "ruckle of bones." He kept on walking even though it was hell to put shoes over his bleeding and ulcerated feet. But because he kept on walking, he was able to explore all of Africa and he thus opened up a new continent to the Western world. You could say that unlike the others who walked the soils of Africa, Livingston stayed the course five minutes longer.

So when it comes to the difference maker in ordinary people achieving greatness, it rests on their doing ordinary things in a persevering way. It rests on doing ordinary things five minutes longer than anybody else.

And beside it being a difference maker when it comes to achieving greatness, it's also the difference maker when it comes to achieving success. There is a story of a young boxer in Australia which brings both a smile and makes a point. He was in a prizefight with a strong opponent. After the fight, he telegraphed his father. The telegram read: "Dear Dad: Won easily in 84 rounds." The fact of winning "easily" after 84 rounds brings a smile but the point is: "Can you imagine the perseverance in going over 84 rounds to win a fight?" Time and again it's been shown and proved that perseverance is the price to be paid for success. Success comes to those willing to stay the course five minutes longer.

A study was conducted by the National Retail Dry Goods Association in regard to the conduct of people in the sales world. Forty-eight percent of all salespeople make one call and then cross off the prospect as a potential customer. Twenty-five percent will do that after the second call. Fifteen percent will cross out the prospect on the third call. While twelve percent will not cross out the prospect at all but will keep going back to them over and over again. It turns out that those twelve percent account for over eighty percent of all the new sales the company will make.

Napoleon Hill, the famous motivator, found that people usually achieve their greatest success one step beyond what would appear to be their greatest failure. It was when every outward indication suggested that it be wise to quit; it was then that they were the very closest to breaking through to their hopeful goal.

I read of an interesting statistic that came out of a study that took place at the University of Rhode Island. Of the 300 subjects who made New Year's resolutions and were still keeping them two years later, nearly all of them averaged 14 lapses before finally maintaining their resolution.

So what appears to account for success in an overwhelming majority of cases rests in one's going 84 rounds. It rests on making call after call after call. It rests on bouncing back time after time after time. It rests on one's doing what they're doing five minutes longer.

And then there's the matter of integrity. One of the greatest works of art is entitled "Angelus." Jean Francois Millet painted it. Millet came close to never finishing that painting because he was beset by the rigors of poverty and he questioned the worthwhileness of going on. He was so poor that he did not have the means to buy fuel for his apartment and, to make matters worse, his mother got sick and died and he couldn't raise the funds necessary to visit her on her deathbed nor to attend the funeral. This triggered an overwhelming feeling of despair and Millet began to contemplate suicide.

While in that depressed state and condition, he drew a sketch of an artist lying dead at the foot of his easel and, as he gazed at that sketch, he heard a woman's voice crying out, "Suicide marks dishonor!" That awakened in him his need to be true to himself and his profession. It alerted him to the importance of maintaining his integrity. So he hung in despite the pressure against his doing so and he went on to finish that painting and continued to stand tall as a painter till he died a natural death.

I recall a character in AJ. Cronin's *The Citadel*[10]. That character was a physician who stood for and lived the ideals of his profession. He was keenly sensitive to human needs. He was eager to be of service and the amount of remuneration was of no concern to him. But then things happened. Difficulties began to mount. Problems began to rise. Troubles became overwhelming. And that physician no longer persevered in those ideals with which he began. He started to partake in actions unbecoming a physician. Unlike Jean Francois Millet, he didn't stay true to himself and his profession. He couldn't stay the course five minutes longer.

No matter what profession we choose in life, be it our work profession or family profession, there are many lures away from the ideals of those professions. There are many life conditions pushing us in the direction of despair and apathy and cynicism. It isn't easy holding fast to ideals for which we may have once stood, but if we can and if we do, if we can go that five minutes longer, we'll maintain our honor and our dignity and we'll have peace in our hearts knowing that we haven't compromised our integrity.

So going five minutes longer can be the difference maker when it comes to greatness, when it comes to achieving success, when it comes to integrity, and also when it comes to a needed change in our life.

According to psychologist Ivan Pavlov, it takes 21 days for anyone to develop and embrace a new habit. Move your wastepaper basket from one side of the desk to another and you'll find yourself dropping papers on the floor for 21 days and on the 22nd day you'll finally get it right as to where the wastepaper basket now happens to be.

People in new homes or in new jobs usually find that it takes about three weeks before they feel comfortable in their new surroundings. Amputees have found that it takes about 21 days for them to realize that their limb is missing. And what holds true for getting used to something new holds true as well for something old. Refrain from a habit for 21 days and there's a good chance of being rid of that habit forever.

Whether one buys the 21-day theory or not, the truth is that any change we hope to make when it comes to our lives demands perseverance. Any variance when it comes to our conduct calls for daily regiments of a particular behavior. Any halt to negative activity requires persistent vigilance. Change is indeed within our means but it requires that we stay the course for 21 days or 22 days or whatever, it requires that we stay the course five minutes longer.

And then, finally, perseverance can be the difference maker when it comes to our survival amidst the trials and tribulations of life. There's a story about a donkey who fell into an old abandoned well. A farmer comes by and, upon seeing him there, makes an effort to secure his rescue. He gathers together a group of men who tried in vain to loop a rope over the donkey. Other strategy was devised but it proved fruitless. Finally, they said, "This donkey isn't worth saving!" and to put it out of its misery they started to shovel dirt into the well. The donkey, now fearing for his life, kept shaking the dirt from his back and, as he did so, he also stepped up. And so it went shovel after shovel after shovel and, finally, the donkey was standing inches from the top of the well and he stepped out of it to safety.

Someone who had observed what had happened said to another: "That's a pretty good lesson for surviving the difficult times of life. All it takes is a daily regiment of shaking it off and stepping up. It may eventually lead to a better day."

No matter how difficult a situation can become, no matter how bad things can get, no matter how much dirt gets tossed our way, survival is within our means. It rests in our not giving up and our not despairing.

It rests on our shaking it off and stepping up. We could well find ourselves walking out of the hell our life may be in but it requires our staying the course five minutes longer.

By now I assume that all of you know that, when I reference five minutes longer, I'm not referring to a clock but I'm referring to perseverance. I'm referring to persistence far beyond the normal and the average. I'm referring to staying the course when all indications are that quitting is the wiser course of action. The widow in the Gospel today did precisely that and it was before a judge who would normally pay no attention to her plea. Thanks to her going five minutes longer, she won the day and secured the decision she so desperately wanted.

And so it can go with us. If we stay the course five minutes longer, it could well be the difference between mediocrity and greatness, between our being a Columbus or our being just an ordinary mariner. If we stay the course five minutes longer, it could well be the difference between failure and success, between our winning or losing that reluctant customer. If we stay the course five minutes longer, it could well be the difference between honor or dishonor, between our being a Jean Francois Millet or our being that physician in Cronin's book *The Citadel*. If we stay the course five minutes longer, it could well be the difference between change or stagnation, between gaining a positive habit or maintaining a bad one. If we stay the course five minutes longer, it could well be the difference between getting buried or freed, between surviving or succumbing to the troubles life will often provide. My friends stay the course five minutes longer. It can make all the difference in the world.

Playing It Safe

Scripture Lesson: Matthew 10: 37-42
"…Whoever finds his life will lose it, and whoever loses his life for my sake will find it…"

A look at what you'll miss should your life be free of risk.

A backwoods farmer, sitting on the steps of his tumbledown shack and chewing on a stem of grass, was approached by a stranger who stopped for a drink of water. Wishing to be sociable, the stranger engaged the farmer in conversation. "How was your cotton crop this year?" he asked.

"Didn't plant none!" said the farmer. "Afraid of the boll weevil!"

"Well," said the stranger, "how's your wheat crop doing?"

"Didn't plant none!" said the farmer. "Afraid it wouldn't rain enough!"

"Well then," asked the stranger, "how's the corn doing?"

"Didn't plant none!" said the farmer. "Afraid of the corn blight!"

"Then what on earth did you plant?" said the stranger.

"I didn't plant nothing!" said the farmer. "I just played it safe!"

I begin with that humorous story because I'd like to talk with you about the hazards of playing it safe. Just as that farmer had an empty field because he chose to play it safe, so too will we have an empty life should we choose to do the same, should we choose to take no risks. There is much we stand to lose when the element of risk plays no part in our life.

For one thing, we'll lose out on a lot of opportunities. I liked that Frank and Ernest comic strip which I happened to see one day. One character says to the other: "Opportunity knocked once but by the time I switched off the alarm system, removed the safety bar, loosened the guard chain, and unlocked the dead bolt; it had gone away!"

Opportunities afford little time for the weighing of risks. So if we happen to be someone who always plays it safe, we've more than likely missed out on a few golden opportunities to better our life, to repair our life, to grow our life; and the sad thing is that those opportunities will probably never come knocking at our door again.

Another hazard of playing it safe is that it tends to guarantee mediocrity. The late Woody Hayes once gave a talk where he noted the difference between All-Americans and also rans and he used a defensive back as his prime example. He told how, when the ball is snapped in a football game, the defensive back has one of two choices when the quarterback goes back to pass. He can choose to play it safe and simply stay behind the receiver so as to make the tackle after the catch. Or, said Woody Hayes, he can choose to position himself so he can step between the receiver and the football at precisely the right moment and make the interception. The first choice minimizes risk while the second choice maximizes risk but, if you look at all the defensive backs who've been named All-Americans, who excelled at that position, they were the ones who had multiple interceptions, they were the ones who chose not to play it safe.

As many of you know, I spent many of my younger years coaching baseball and one of the things I always look for in a player was their willingness to charge the ball, their willingness to dive at balls they could have let go by. That style of play heightened the risk for an error, but it also placed them a cut above the player who merely stood their ground and waited for the ball to come to them.

The dividing line, the difference maker between mediocrity and excellence rests on the issue of playing it safe. Those playing it safe never put themselves in a position where excellence can be achieved and so mediocrity becomes the foregone conclusion.

The third hazard of playing it safe is that it can guarantee our misery. Thomas Ogletree says that one of the most significant moments in the civil rights movement occurred in 1962 when a group of black students held a service of repentance for the sin of acquiescence. According to Ogletree, this service marked the realization that as bad as white racism happened to be, it was not the whole problem. Blacks had been willing in many instances to deny their humanity and to let others make all their decisions for them and it was this willingness to relinquish freedom that was as much a piece of their lack of civil-rights as was the racism of the white community.

When Eric Fromm was a young psychiatrist in Berlin, Germany in the 1920s and '30s, he watched with amazement Hitler's rise to power and he would write later that one of the main contributors to that rise was the willingness of the German people to give up their freedom. And that was due in large measure to their desire for comfort and security.

Be it the observations of Thomas Ogletree or the observations of Eric Fromm, it's not unusual to find that people will relinquish freedom and even remain as slaves because it's a whole lot safer and a lot more secure than dealing with the unknown which might otherwise lie before them. There are risks that need to be taken should we choose to end our misery. There's insecurity involved should we wish to change the sad way in which we're presently living our lives. And so if we're prone to playing it safe, we'll more than likely take a pass on our doing what's necessary and needed to escape the mess our lives may happen to be in.

The fourth hazard of playing it safe is it will mean kissing greatness good-bye. In Robert Bolt's drama, *The Man for All Seasons*, Sir Thomas More is Chancellor to the King of England. He finds himself caught in the tension between his legal commitment to be loyal to King Henry VIII and his faith commitment to be loyal to God and the Church. He realized that the former afforded him safety and security while the latter did not. Courageously he chooses the latter and, as a result, More is thrown into jail and then later executed by the King. The play is powerful and it's based upon a true story. And if today you'd inquire as to the names of some of the greatest figures in English history, the name of Thomas More would most certainly be listed.

Greatness doesn't usually carry with it a death sentence but it does carry with it a lot of risk. To walk where great people have walked involves the abandoning of any hope of safety or security. If Christopher Columbus chose safety and security over risk, he'd never have left the harbors of Spain. If Martin Luther King Jr. chose safety and security over risk, he'd have never left the pulpit of the Ebenezer Baptist Church. If the Wright Brothers chose safety and security over risk, they'd have listened to their dad and have quit "their foolish airship experiments." If Jesus chose safety and security over risk, he'd have never entered Jerusalem and there would be no crucifixion and there would be no resurrection. If we have any aspirations towards greatness, there is no playing it safe when it comes to our dreams, our hopes, or our ambitions.

The fifth hazard of playing it safe is its potential for loneliness and regret. One of the most painful movies I've ever viewed starred Anthony Hopkins in the role of a butler named Stevens. The movie was entitled *Remains of the Day*. The butler Stevens had come from a long line of butlers and so was well-disciplined and very prim and proper, but also very detached from life with few if any relationships. The household for which he worked hires a housekeeper. Her name was Miss Kenton. She was vivacious as well as beautiful and not long thereafter Stevens becomes infatuated with her. He'd like nothing more than to strike up a relationship with her but the problem was, and this was the painful part of the movie, the problem was that he wouldn't take the risk of revealing his feelings towards her. He wouldn't drop his guard and disclose to Miss Kenton that behind the facade of a prim and proper butler was a man who was deeply in love with her. She'd eventually leave that household and, much to the pain and consternation of Stevens, marry someone else.

There are many people much like that Hopkins character in *Remains of the Day*. They'd like to reach out to others. They'd like to establish a friendship. They'd like to break free from their loneliness. But they're afraid to take the risk of being rejected. They're afraid to take the risk of dropping their guard and revealing to someone what it is that happens to lie deep within their heart. That fear of risk-taking, that unwillingness to step out from the safety and security of their guarded life will often find them in a similar predicament to that of the butler Stevens. It will find them bemoaning the loss of a love or a friendship that they could well have had while at the same time finding themselves still beset with the yearning to be free of loneliness.

The sixth hazard of playing it safe is that we may never come to know the beauty and the excitement that life has the ability to provide. Not long ago, in a segment of television's *60 Minutes*, Mike Wallace was interviewing one of the Sherpa guides from Nepal. They're the guides climbers hire to help them reach the peak of Mount Everest. "Why do it?" Wallace asked him. "To help others do something they cannot do on their own!" was the reply. "But there are so many risks, so many dangers!" said Wallace. "Why do you continue to take people to the top of the mountain?" The Sherpa guide smiled and said: "Mr. Wallace, it's obvious that you've never been to the top."

Anyone bent on safety and security never knows what it's like to have been to the top. They'll never know the exhilaration of a difficult goal achieved. They'll never know the excitement of a beautiful dream fulfilled. They'll never know the satisfaction of a realized ambition. And that's because the risks and dangers which those goals and dreams and ambitions would require are not within their comfort zone, a zone they're not wont to leave.

And finally, the seventh hazard of playing it safe is the missed chance to be a fool for Christ's sake. You've heard me tell you many times of the story of Jean Valjean from Victor Hugo's *Les Misérables*. The turning point of Valjean's life comes when he's released from prison after being confined there for years for stealing a mere loaf of bread. Wandering about aimlessly, he finds himself in the company of a Bishop who welcomes him into his home. Valjean is there but a night when he decides to run off with the silver candlesticks that had adorned the Bishop's dining room table. Within minutes, he's apprehended by the police and hauled back to the Bishop's residence, candlesticks in hand. To Valjean's shock and surprise, the Bishop informs the police that he had given Valjean the candlesticks as a gift and they should therefore release him immediately.

When you think about it, what that Bishop did for Valjean was not exactly the safest or the wisest thing he could have done. Valjean could have continued to steal and that would have sullied the Bishop's reputation. He'd have been seen and labeled a fool for being so forgiving. But that's often the case with any granting of forgiveness, with any break that's given, with any chance that's taken when it comes to someone whom we're not sure is deserving of the risk we took on their behalf.

And that's often the case as well with going out on a limb for some cause or some ideal which very few happen to share or some dream few believe to be feasible. There's risk attached to our doing such things, there's insecurity attached in our making moves that bold but, as we saw in *Les Miserables*, it can bear great fruit. And even if it doesn't, even if it results in our being branded a fool; we'd be a fool for Christ's sake and that, my friends, is an honor.

There's a line in today's Gospel that we've all heard many times. It's the words of Jesus: "Those who find their life will lose it and those who lose their life for my sake will find it." Putting it another way: "Whoever secures their life will lose it and whoever risks their life will find it." In essence Jesus is telling us that it's not wise to play it safe.

My friends, there are obviously times when we must be prudent and must play it safe, but to do so always, to constantly choose safety and security over risk is a hazard and a detriment to a full and beautiful life.

We may miss a golden opportunity that will never come by again. We'll be mired in mediocrity and never achieve the excellence within our reach. Greatness will be out of the question and we can pretty much count on staying lonely and miserable and we may well miss out on the beauty and excitement life can offer. And we'll never get to wear the badge of honor for being a fool for Christ's sake.

The farmer in the opening story decided to play it safe and, as a result, had an empty field. Be wary about playing it safe! It may result in an empty life!

Disconnection

Scripture Lesson: Matthew 23: 1-12
"...For they preach but do not practice..."

When the word "disconnection" is applied to people, it's not a very nice thing.

The word disconnection packs a pretty negative wallop. Internet users aren't at all pleased to see a form of that word appear on their computer screens. Cell phone users sigh when a weak battery disconnects them from a call they desperately needed to complete and television watchers do the same when a bad storm disconnects their set from its cable feed. And then there's the most horrid of all encounters with the word and that's when a doctor sadly informs you that your loved one needs to be disconnected from a respirator. Whenever we encounter some version of the word disconnection, a negative chord is struck and much grimacing and pain will often follow.

That's especially true when the word is applied to people. Consider those Nazi guards in Hitler's concentration camps. In many a camp, they were responsible for organizing an opera company, an opera company of gifted singers and wonderful musicians all of whom happened to be prisoners. And when those guards would sit and listen to a performance of that company, tears would be streaming down their face so moved were they by the performance. Those very same

97

guards, who were cultured and educated, who appreciated and loved the beauty of excellent music as well as the work of the operatic masters, those very same guards on the very next day were putting women and little children into gas chambers.

Some of you might recall the movie and the play called *Death and the Maiden*[11] where the physician's job in the prison camp was to keep prisoners alive so they could be tortured more, to keep them, in essence, on the living side of death. During all this time, you would see him listening to Franz Schubert's exquisite masterpiece *Death and the Maiden* with tears streaming down his face.

In that physician as well as in those Nazi guards, you have an unbelievable disconnection between one's outer life and one's inner life, between one's external demeanor and one's internal demeanor, between one's inner elegance and one's outer elegance. It's hard to believe such a disconnection can exist but it does and when it does, as was the case in Nazi Germany, it strikes not just a negative chord but it strikes a demonic chord and the intensity of the grimacing and the pain is immense. When "disconnection" is applied to people, it's not a very nice thing.

When Theodore Parker, the great New England writer, was a little child, he saw in the garden a turtle and he lifted his hand to strike it but something checked his arm. He heard a voice within him say that it was wrong for him to strike that turtle. When he went back to the house, he asked his mother who it was that said it was wrong to strike the turtle. Taking him into her arms, his mother told him that some call it "conscience" while she sees it as "the voice of God emanating from one's soul." She then went on to tell him: "Son, if you listen to and obey that voice, it will speak to you clearer and clearer and it will guide you along the paths of righteousness and of truth."

Unfortunately, there are many no longer hearing God's voice emanating from their souls, many who in one way or another have disconnected themselves from their conscience. They will do wrong things. They will behave in an unethical manner. They will cheat and lie and exhibit all sorts of reprehensible behavior, all the while not experiencing the least bit of guilt or shame. Although not quite as demonic as the disconnection of those Nazi guards, the disconnection they exhibit also strikes a negative chord and usually unbeknownst to them, an onslaught of grimacing as well as pain. When "disconnection" is applied to people, it's not a very nice thing.

And then you have the disconnection responsible for so much of the apathy in existence in our world today. John Woolman's Journal is one of the classic spiritual journals and in one part of it Woolman mournfully writes of a trip during which he visited Quaker groups in North Carolina. He found as he went through the minutes of their meetings a series of words which kept appearing and which disturbed him very much. Those words were: "No business that required entry or action." Woolman wrote: "In God's name, with the sin of slavery all around them, with all the warmongering going on between the North and South, how could they possibly write 'no business that required entry or action'!"

There are many today just like those Quakers who so upset John Woolman. There are many today who appear to be totally disconnected from the world around them, totally disconnected from the troubles and the cruelties and the prejudice and the bigotry that plagues so many of the people near whom they happen to live. From them, you hear no cries of protest, no shouts of concern, even though there are all sorts of injustices, all sorts of horrific things going on all around them.

And then right alongside that kind of disconnection is the one that disconnects "us" from "them," one that doesn't see certain people and certain lives as valuable or important.

Not too long ago, the New York Times relegated the deaths of several hundred people in West Bengal to a half column on page 11 of their newspaper. A Network news program some months back led the news with an economic report and stories related to unemployment. Some 10 minutes later, they reported on the crash of an Ethiopian airliner with hundreds of people on board. The headline of a story in the Manchester Guardian told of a disaster in the far East in which hundreds upon hundreds were killed and billions upon billions of dollars worth of property damaged. The headline read: "Manchester man injured abroad."

One's disconnection from people of other lands and languages is often helped along by the national media. We're given the sense that "ours" are the only lives that matter, that however horrid may be the news and the living conditions of people in the Third World, it pales in comparison to what is happening to "us." That disconnection not only strikes a negative chord, but the apathy it breeds is one of the reasons why poverty and famine and exploitation continue to go unabated resulting in the grimacing and the pain of many living in lesser lands and lesser nations. When "disconnection" is applied to people, it's not a very nice thing.

And then you have the disconnection responsible for so many unhappy and unfulfilled lives. When Henry David Thoreau was about eight years old, a visitor in his home asked him what he wanted to be when he grows up. Young Thoreau replied with great solemnity: "I want to be I." Unfortunately, unlike Thoreau, many when asked that question say: "I want to be someone else." "I want to be this person or that person" and, as a result, their lives get disconnected from who they really are and what they're really all about.

I read recently a few interesting tidbits from Hollywood history. When Charlie Chaplin started making films, the director of the pictures insisted on Chaplin imitating a popular German comedian of that day. Charlie Chaplin got nowhere until he shunned that imitation and started being himself. Bob Hope had a similar experience. He spent years doing a song and dance routine that went nowhere until he began making wisecracks, until he began being himself. Will Rogers twirled a rope in vaudeville for years without saying a word. He gets nowhere until he discovered in himself a unique gift of humor and that prompted him to talk while twirling his rope. When Gene Autry got rid of his Texas accent and dressed like a city boy and claimed he was from New York, people laughed behind his back. But when he started twanging his banjo and singing cowboy ballads, as he was wont to do, Gene Autry embarked on a career that made him the world's most popular cowboy. When Chaplin, Hope, Rogers, and Autry chose to be "I" instead of choosing to be "somebody else," their lives underwent a transformation and they were spared an unhappy and an unfulfilled life.

There are many people today who are anything but themselves, who are living a life tailored for someone their parents may have suggested that they be. And that disconnection from their "I," that disconnection from who they really are finds them leading a life that's less than it could be and one that really isn't their own.

So when it comes to disconnection striking a negative chord, when it comes to disconnection causing grimacing and pain, there's the disconnection of ones outer life from one's inner life. There's the disconnection from one's conscience, the disconnection from the problems and issues of people other than "our own," the disconnection from one's true self, and finally there's the disconnection of one's emotional life from one's rational life.

Howard K. Smith wrote a book entitled *Last Train from Berlin*[12] and in it he describes the stunning spectacles which Hitler used to stage in the 1930s. There were columns of marching bands, all sorts of paraphernalia, soldiers marching in unison, flags of every sort and variety. It stirred in him all sorts of excitement. He said: "my hair stood on end." Then, after a while, he said: "My brain muscled in. I remembered just what it was I had viewed. It was not a stunning spectacle but it was an obscene spectacle orchestrated by a madman and I hadn't noticed that till my brain muscled into my emotions."

Many times, I'm afraid, not unlike Howard K. Smith we get taken up by our emotions, we allow certain feelings to occupy all of our attention, and if our "brain doesn't muscle in," if somehow our emotional side gets disconnected from our rational side, we could find ourselves doing or believing what should have been resisted, doing or believing what is silly and foolish and bad. Many a murder has been committed. Many a tragic mistake has occurred. Many a horrible decision has been made. All because the "brain never had a chance to muscle in," all because one's feelings got disconnected from one's wisdom. When "disconnection" is applied to people, it's not a very nice thing.

I've been making a case today for the evils and tragedies of disconnection because disconnection is the center point of our Gospel. It's the reason Jesus sounded so upset when he talked about the

Pharisees. He wasn't at all pleased with the fact that their actions never backed their words. He wasn't at all pleased that their internal demeanor was disconnected from their external demeanor. Jesus was upset because no connection existed between what they taught and how they acted, between what they said and how they lived.

So the call of the Gospel is for us to check our disconnections. To check if our outer elegance is connected with our inner elegance. To check if our conscience is connected to our actions. To check if who we are is connected to the "I" within us. To check if our concern and interest is connected to people other than those in our immediate circle. To check if our brain is connected to our feelings. If there are any disconnections, it's time we put together what should never have been put asunder. Our doing so will help lessen a lot of grimacing as well as a lot of pain.

Closing the Gate

Scripture Lesson: Philippians 3: 8-14
"...I give no thought to what lies behind..."

Many things are past history and they need to be forgotten.

Dr. Tom Tewell, who is pastor of the Fifth Avenue Presbyterian Church in New York, recently told of a tradition kept to this day at the Culver Military Academy. At their graduation exercise, the cadets, one by one, walk across the stage, receive their diplomas, shake hands with the President of the Academy and then they symbolically walk through an archway into their future. As they do so, one of the academy officers shouts the command: "Don't forget to close the gate!" The command is made to remind the graduates that, before they walk into their futures, they need to close the gate on their past.

I reference that Culver Military Academy tradition because I'd like to talk with you today about closing the gate, about putting behind you all from your past that can seriously impede your future. There are many things we need to remember but there are also many things we need to forget and the quicker we're able to forget certain things from our past, the better will be our futures, the better will be our lives.

We need first to close the gate on the hurts and pains we may have suffered from someone who may have once had a claim on our love. One of my favorite anecdotes from the works of Rabbi Harold Kushner involves his counseling a wife and mother whose husband had left her for another woman many years before. She had come to see the Rabbi because her "no good husband" had fallen behind on his child support payments thus adding fuel to the fire of her growing resentment. When she finished ranting and raving about her ex-husband, Kushner offered an interesting suggestion. He suggested that she forgive him, that she put his reprehensible behavior behind her. The woman couldn't believe what the rabbi was asking and queried as to how she could possibly forgive him and forget about all he had done to her and her children. Kushner had a good response. He said: "I'm not asking you to forgive him because what he did wasn't all that bad. What he did was terrible. I'm asking you to forgive him and to put his behavior behind you because he does not deserve to have the power to turn you into a bitter and resentful woman."

When the hurts we're suffering have been inflicted upon us by someone we once loved, they are particularly painful more so than any other hurt and it tends to fire up the embers of bitterness and resentment like nothing else can. For the reason Kushner presented and for the sake of relief from the sting of those embers of bitterness and resentment, it behooves us to close the gate on what it was we suffered at the hands of someone we once loved.

It also behooves us to close the gate as well on whatever it is we may have suffered at the hands of someone we may have never loved. President Clinton often spoke of his first meeting Nelson Mandela. In his conversation with that great leader of South Africa, Clinton told Mandela of how he happened to be watching television on the day he was released from prison and happened to catch the footage of his walk from his cell to the gates of the prison. Clinton told how the camera had settled on his face and Clinton recounted as to how he had never seen a face that glowed with as much anger and hatred as did his that day.

Mandela was surprised that Clinton had caught that on television that night. "I have to admit," said Mandela, "that I did seethe with anger and rage and hatred as I walked through that prison yard because all I kept thinking of was all that my enemy had taken from me. Then," he said, "as I neared the gate I heard an inner voice say:

'Nelson, for 27 years you were their prisoner but you were always a free man. Don't allow your enemy to make you into a free man only to turn you into their prisoner!'" Nelson Mandela heeded that inner voice and closed the gate on the hurts imposed on him by his enemies and what a blessing to the world he's become.

Mandela's inner voice captured one of the best reasons for forgetting past hurts and that's its severance from its poison. Too many leave the clutches of their enemy only to take on the very qualities that they hated in their enemy. To be spared that fate, to keep us from exhibiting the poison they injected into our systems, it's imperative that we shut the gate on any hurt or pain that got imposed on us by our enemy, imposed on us by someone we have never loved.

And it's also imperative as well that we close the gate on the bad experiences which may have littered our past. Several years ago there was a Peanuts cartoon that got published just after the first of the year. The strip involved Lucy and Charlie Brown having a conversation about New Year's resolutions. Charlie tells Lucy how for the New Year he's resolved to set new goals for himself. He was going to forget all about last year and start anew. He was going to put his past failures behind him and really go out and accomplish something significant in the year ahead. Lucy lets out one of her "Umps!" and tells Charlie how it's never going to work, how she tried to do that last year but failed. "What I'm going to do this year," says Lucy to Charlie, "what I'm going to do this year is regret. I'm going to cry over spilled milk. I'm going to cry over lost loves. I'm going to cry over broken dreams." Says Lucy to Charlie: "This is going to be my year to do nothing but regret."

Unfortunately, there are a lot of us doing as Lucy resolved to do. There are a lot of us crying over spilled milk, crying over lost loves, crying over broken dreams. It's imperative that we close the gate on those bad experiences for not to do so dooms us to a very unhappy life.

Thankfully for him as well as for us, one of the great minds of the 20th century came to that very conclusion, that very realization. I'm referring to Buckminster Fuller. At the age of 32, he was about as low as anybody can get. He was bankrupt and unemployed with a wife and a new baby to support and he was still reeling over the loss of that baby's older sister who had just died a few months earlier. The weight of all that misery found him drinking heavily. It was then that he decided to cast aside the past, to shut the gate on all the bad experiences which had been weighing heavily upon his soul. In the following 56 years, he became an architect, an inventor, an author and one of the most widely respected men in the entire world. He wrote 28 books, received 44 honorary degrees; he won 25 patents and literally changed the way human beings think. Buckminster Fuller could have spent his life regretting, he could have spent his life bemoaning what had been lost but instead he put his bad experiences behind him and, as a result, a new and a great life was born.

So it can go with us. There may indeed be a new and great life awaiting us as well but we'll never know if we choose to do as Lucy resolved to do. We'll never know until the gate gets closed on the bad experiences in our past and we move on with our lives.

And besides the bad experiences, it may be imperative as well to close the gate on the good experiences of life. There are many anecdotes associated with the life of Alexander the Great but the one that's proved most interesting occurred at the end of an excursion where he and his men recorded a whole series of conquests. The group was scheduled to return to Greece and they had in their possession large supplies of booty gained from the lands they had conquered. They were about to begin the march home when Alexander made the announcement that he would be taking nothing back to Greece, that what he really desired was not souvenirs from the past but more adventures, more possibilities for a greater life and an even greater record of achievements. To make his point, he ordered kerosene to be poured over all the wagons of his share of the booty. Then he personally set a flame to the kerosene. The action had a dramatic effect upon his soldiers. Incredibly, they, too, poured kerosene over their share of the booty and set fire to it as well. Then instead of marching home, Alexander and his army marched off to new lands, new conquests, and new adventures.

Now, I'm not suggesting that we need destroy everything we earned in our many years of hard work but I am suggesting that there comes a time when we need to do as Alexander did, when we need to shut the gate on past successes and past accomplishments and quit resting on our laurels. There comes a time when we need to examine what else God may have in store for us and our life, that we need to explore what new challenges and new opportunities may be standing before us beckoning our response.

So when it comes to closing the gate as we walk into our futures, there's a need to close the gate on past hurts and pains; there's a need to close the gate on the bad experiences of our life; there's a need to close the gate on the good experiences of our life; and there's also a need to close the gate on the sins we may have committed long ago.

Two brothers were once convicted of stealing sheep and, in accordance with the brutal punishment of that day, they were branded on their foreheads with the letters "S T" that stood for sheep thief. One of the brothers, unable to bear the stigma, left home and wandered aimlessly from land to land and, full of regret and bitterness, met an early death and was buried in a forgotten grave. The other brother did just the opposite. He did not go away from home. He said: "I can't run away from the fact that I stole sheep, but I can put it behind me and start a new life!" And so he stayed close to home and did what he could to win back the respect of his neighbors as well as himself. As years passed, he performed many a good deed and gradually gained a reputation for respectability and honesty. One day a stranger in the town saw the old man with the letters S T branded on his forehead and he asked a native of the town as to what that signified. After thinking for a while, the villager said: "It all happened a great while ago and I've forgotten the particulars but I think the letters are an abbreviation for saint."

No matter how grave a sin we may have committed; no matter how bad an act we may have performed; no matter how terrible a deed we may have done; the beauty of our faith is that God's forgiveness is there for us to embrace as is the grace to change and transform its scarring effect. Along with that embracing, there comes the necessity of our closing the gate on that sin or deed or act. As one of the great saints of the church once said: "What God has forgotten, tis no business of ours to remember." And whatever branding may still be in evidence, we have a future ahead of us to alter and transform it.

The apostle Paul knew full well the importance of closing the gate and moving on. He told us in our second reading that he sees himself straining forward to what lies ahead but that's only after forgetting what lies behind. Paul knew full well that as wonderful as it is to remember, it's also good and wonderful to forget, to shut the gate on certain things embedded in our past.

Like shutting the gate on those hurts and slights inflicted upon us by those we once loved thus keeping them from turning us into a bitter and resentful person. Like shutting the gate on those slights and hurts that have come from those we never loved thus keeping their poison from infecting our lives. Like shutting the gate on the bad experiences of our life so like Buckminster Fuller, a new and greater life may be born. Like shutting the gate on the good experiences of life so, like Alexander the Great, new adventures may be experienced. Like shutting the gate on our sins so we won't let its branding send us to a forgotten grave.

That's a great tradition they have at Culvert Military Academy. May we adopt it as a ritual for our life.

The Voice of God

Scripture Lesson: John 10: 27-32
"...My sheep hear my voice..."

God's voice comes in various shapes, forms and colors.

A young child was caught red handed stealing cookies from a cookie jar. The following dialogue took place between her and her mom: "Did you know that God was present when you stole those cookies?"

"Yes, Mom."

"Did you know he was looking at you all the time?"

"Yes, Mom."

"And what did you think he was saying to you?"

"Well, Mom, when I put my hand in the cookie jar I heard God's voice and he was saying to me: 'There's no one here but the two of us so take two.'"

I reference that humorous story because I'd like to talk with you about the voice of God, in particular, the manner in which God speaks. That little girl may have stretched the truth a bit when it came to hearing God's voice, but the fact is, God's voice can and does get heard.

Sometimes it's heard in the form of a scream or a cry or a whimper. Whitaker Chambers is not a name you'd be familiar with but he was a journalist for the *New York Times*. In his autobiography, he recounts a conversation he had with a daughter of a former German diplomat who tried to explain why her father had withdrawn his support of Stalin and Communist rule. She told Whitaker that her father had been friends with Stalin and believed that all the bad said about him were nothing but a set of lies. "Then," she said, "then one night in Moscow he heard screams in the vicinity of Stalin's men. It was then that he realized that what was said about Stalin were not lies at all."

Many times God's voice can take the form of just such screams. They can take the form of cries of anguish. They can take the form of whimpers of pain and suffering. As Jesus told us, God tends to incarnate in those that are persecuted, those that are treated unjustly, those who are devoid of the bare necessities of life. And I would surmise that whenever we hear a cry or a scream or a whimper from one of those least of our brothers or sisters, we hear the voice of God.

I was in Washington D.C. but a few weeks ago and visited a place called the Newseum. It's a museum which takes you through the history of news-telling, going all the way back to the papyrus days of ancient Egypt. They had on display the Pulitzer prize-winning photographs taken over the past 10 years. The one that truly struck me and moved me was one of a little boy huddled over the ground, an obvious victim of starvation. Twenty feet behind him, standing on the ground, was a vulture waiting for his death to occur. No sound accompanied it but the voice of God. It bellowed out of that photograph.

So, first of all, God's voice can take the form of a scream or cry or sometimes just the image of someone in utter desperation. Secondly, God's voice can also echo from reminders that we're not as smart or as important or as perfect as we think ourselves to be.

I always liked that story of a large truck that wedged itself beneath an underpass outside a small town. It couldn't move forward and it couldn't move backwards. Traffic was backed up for miles. Experts were called to the scene and no one could figure how to free the truck. As they huddled together to explore some possible options, a little boy who had been observing the scene came up to the experts and told them that he knew how to free the truck. The men laughed but then they stopped laughing when the boy suggested they let air out of the truck's tires. They did so and the truck was freed. Having observed what took place, someone remarked that the truck was not the only one who got some air taken out of its tires.

I'm reminded of a conversation a cardinal had with the pastor of the church in which he was about to preach. The cardinal looked out at the congregation and remarked as to how the congregation looked a bit thin. "Didn't you tell them I was coming?" he said to the pastor. "No, I didn't!" the pastor replied. "But you know how things get out."

Many times we get hit between the eyes by a remark that cuts us down to size, a statement that brings our ego down a couple of notches. We tend sometimes to believe that we are the cat's meow, that we are the holders of these vast amounts of knowledge. We tend sometimes to believe that when we were made they threw the mold away. But every once in awhile via someone like that little boy or someone like that pastor, every once in awhile God speaks and we're humbled. We're faced with the reality of our imperfection and our limitations.

So God's voice gets heard in the form of screams or cries. It gets heard in the form of statements which expose the fact that we're not as smart or as important as we think ourselves to be. And God's voice gets heard as well in the form of an affirmation of our assets.

Theodore Geisel's art teacher told him he couldn't draw and publishers said he couldn't write. His Dartmouth college fraternity voted him least likely to succeed. And then Geisel received one sentence of praise which was enough to motivate him to continue pursuing his dream of being an illustrator and a writer. That sentence of praise was uttered when Geisel drew a cow with wings and an acrobat's body and a mischievousness expression on its face. "That's a very fine flying cow!" said Helen Palmer, one of his classmates and someone whose opinion he greatly respected.

It could be said that that one line, that one sentence of praise proved to be the voice of God for it would ultimately propel Geisel to write and draw a wonderful series of children's books. Geisel would become none other than Dr. Seuss and that may never have been his destiny had God not chosen to speak through Helen Palmer, had God's voice not uttered those words of praise.

A similar story can be told of Alex Hailey who went through four years of rejections from various publishers till finally he received one letter which had handwritten across the top of it "Nice try." "I almost cried!" said Hailey, "I was moved beyond words." With his resolve now bolstered by that handwritten message, it would be soon thereafter that the novel *Roots* would get published, spawning a marvelous career of writing for Alex Hailey.

In contrast to Doctor Seuss, Hailey heard God's voice in the form of a written word. So be it written or be it vocal, God's voice can be heard whenever affirmation gets delivered, whenever something positive is said of a talent or ability or an asset that may have otherwise gone unnoticed, that may have otherwise never seen the light of day.

And God's voice can also be heard in the utterance of a truth hard and difficult to swallow. One of the great plays of all time centered on the life of a true man of integrity, Sir Thomas More. It was entitled *A Man for All Seasons*. In one scene, Sir Thomas finds himself imprisoned and sentenced to die all because of a lie told by Richard Rich, a worm of a man, who saw the lie as a means for self-promotion. Shortly thereafter, thanks to the lie, Rich would be appointed the Attorney General of Wales. More happens to see Richard Rich walk by his cell wearing a medal signifying his newly gained office. He reads the inscription "Wales," he said to him: "Richard, Richard, Richard, it profits a man nothing to give his soul for the whole world, but for Wales?" More stung Richard Rich with the truth of his littleness and I'm sure he wasn't the least bit pleased to hear it.

Whenever a remark strikes at someone, exposing the truth of a sin that's an embarrassment to the sinner, it can be seen as the voice of God reminding him or her of something that they can't pretend not to know.

And when God's voice is not exposing the truth of sin, it could very well be exposing the truth of a responsibility. I read recently of a colleague, John Claypool who had been going through a difficult period in his life and was fast becoming a recluse bogged down by self-pity. Referencing that dark period of time, Claypool said that what helped him most was a counselor who hit him with a truth. The counselor said to him point blank: "John, what makes you so special that you should be exempt from pain or suffering or be so gifted and wise that you can avoid it?" He followed that line with a remark: "John when are you going to re-join the human race?" Claypool called that double hit of truth as the beginning of his road to recovery, the beginning of his reentry into ministry.

So whether it be revelatory or confrontational, whether it be referencing a sin or referencing a responsibility, the voice of God resounds in a truth hard and difficult to swallow, yet a truth that needed to be faced.

And finally, God's voice resounds wherever beauty happens to be found. In Jerusalem just as Desert Shield became Desert Storm, Zubin Mehta was conducting the Israel Philharmonic Orchestra. Isaac Stern was the featured soloist. The sirens sounded, warning that a scud missile was on its way. If it were not intercepted, it would most certainly explode releasing who knows what into the air. The members of the audience put on their gas masks and the orchestra left the stage. Fear and trepidation was evident and visible throughout the auditorium. It was then that Isaac Stern crept onto the stage and took a seat and then began to play with his violin John Sebastian Bach's *Serenade for a Solo Violin*. The sound soothed the hearts of the frightened crowd and its beauty trumped the ugliness and wickedness of the tools of war. You could say that the voice of God resounded through that violin played upon that stage.

Whenever there are sounds of beauty, whenever one's ears or one's eyes get filled with something that's beautiful to behold, one is being captivated by the voice of God.

And that I believe is the ultimate gauge by which to determine whether what one is hearing is indeed the voice of God. For be it that scream near Stalin's men or the cry that was captured by that Pulitzer prize-winning photograph; be it the truth John Claypool heard or the truth leveled upon Richard Rich; be it the affirmation of Dr. Seuss' artistic talent or the affirmation of Alex Hailey's writing skill; be it the kids telling the experts to deflate the tires of that truck or the Pastor telling the Cardinal how things have a habit of leaking out; what we're

RICHARD E. ZAJAC

looking at are remarks or statements which have as their result
something beautiful coming life's way through the action or the
change or the facing of the truth on the part of the one doing the
listening. With beauty thus being exposed, the remarks and statements
can indeed be hailed as the voice of God.

Our Gospel today quotes Jesus as saying: "My sheep hear my
voice." My friends, we are God's sheep. Let us keep our ears open
lest we miss the hearing of God's voice.

We're in This Together

Scripture Lesson: Matthew 1: 18-24

"…They shall name him Emmanuel which means 'God is with us.'"

It's too sad of a message for Christmas morning, but an important one for people to hear.

On this day before Christmas, there's excitement in the air. Many young children are filled with anticipation wondering how many of the toys on Santa's list will make it to the bottom of the tree. Many a young damsel's heart will be fluttering wondering whether tonight will be the night her beau will pop the big question. There'll be people heading to the airport hoping that the flight carrying a family member will arrive at the scheduled time. Many a man or woman will be fussing in the kitchen making sure all the traditional food items are properly prepared for the big Christmas meal. Some are scurrying to the mall hoping to buy that one gift that will complete the shopping list. Excitement, exuberance, happiness, and frivolity fill the air.

But, you know, for many that will not be the case. Many will be feeling out of sync with the world this Christmas Eve. There will be those who will be celebrating the day in a hospital bed or in a prison or in some shelter for the homeless. There'll be those who will be with family but they will feel empty inside because a loved one had recently passed away. There will be those who feel a big tear in their heart because they know that this will probably be the last Christmas for a certain ailing member of the family. There will be some who will have a secret hurt that no one knows about but which shall be markedly painful when Christmas finally arrives. There's a good number of people on this Christmas Eve who will feel particularly left out of the joy and excitement and celebrative spirit that are so much a part of this season of the year.

It is to these people, however, that Christmas really speaks because below the surface of all the festivities, all the gift exchanges, and all the decorations of this joyous time, there lies the figure of an infant in a hard and a cold stable, the figure of God choosing right from the very beginning to identify himself with all whose experience of life is hard and cold. The bottom line of Bethlehem can be found in those words: "You shall call him Emmanuel" which means God is with us. The baby born in a stable was to be a sign to all the world that God will forever be at the side of his people, especially those left out of the "Inn," those not privy to the good things and good times of life.

In ancient Palestine and even in some sections of the Eastern world today, farmers often use what is called a training yoke. When a younger, inexperienced animal, such as an ox, is suddenly introduced to the difficult work of plowing a field, he's provided with a training yoke. The yoke was a two-animal harness designed in such a way that the heavier load was placed on the shoulders of a stronger and more experienced animal while the lighter load went to the animal unfamiliar and inexperienced when it came to the task at hand. Thanks to that arrangement, the younger animal could bear the yoke and plow the fields in a far more manageable way.

When God saw his people broken, downtrodden, and hurting, he wanted desperately to help lift the burden, to help his people negotiate the misery they were experiencing. By assuming our human condition, by becoming one like us at Bethlehem, God put himself in a position to experience the difficulties and pains of life. In that way, when we're called upon to plow difficult fields, God's there to occupy the heavier, more experienced side of our training yoke.

The story is told of Dr. Elizabeth Kubler Ross, famous for her work in the field of death and dying. Asked to discuss her findings with students of ministry and the clergy, she told of a small child too young to comprehend the concept of death but still very much aware of the dreadful things happening to him. Since he had difficulty expressing his fears, she asked him to draw a picture of how he felt. The child drew a picture of a house engulfed in flames, the fire licking around the door and windowsill. In front of the burning house stood a stick figure child, a cannon pointed to his head. Dr. Kubler Ross drew the picture on the blackboard in the classroom. She turned to the ministers and students and asked what they thought the boy then drew when asked what he needed the most.

One student surmised that he drew a picture of someone holding up a stop sign. Another thought he'd draw another stick figure with a water hose spraying water on the house and the cannon. Yet another surmised that he'd draw someone pushing the cannon away.

Kubler Ross nodded her head "No!" to all three. Sensing the group was baffled as to the answer; she quietly walked to the blackboard and drew a picture of a stick figure standing beside the boy holding his hand. "That," she said, "was what the boy had drawn to express what he needed the most."

Wanting to be of help when pain and suffering is at its worst or when tragedy strikes, God became one like us. God drew himself into the human picture to let all of us know that when life's got us down, he'll be there to hold our hand, to get us through, to walk at our side as we plow through the ugly fields before us.

I remember hearing of John Sutherland Barnel tell of a visit he had in the hospital with a man who was afraid of all the paraphernalia that was present there. The patient was one of those self-managing individuals who was now at the mercy of a nurse for a cup of water and he didn't like it. He was also under an oxygen tent and it scared him. John Barnel went over to that tent and zipped down the opening and put his head next to his friend's head and said: "Let's breathe this air together."

If Christmas finds you feeling low and down in the dumps and filled with gloom, if Christmas finds you feeling out of sync with everyone else, take heart! Bethlehem was meant for you. Bethlehem was God's way of saying: "Let's breathe this air together!"

Blacksmith's Creed

Scripture Lesson: 1 Corinthians 10:16-17
"…We, though many, are one body…"

We are all interconnected and what we do can have a profound and far reaching effect.

The blacksmiths of old had a creed which was often posted on the walls of their shops. It read as follows: For lack of a nail the shoe is lost, for lack of a shoe, a horse is lost, for lack of a horse the General is lost, for lack of a General the victory is lost, for lack of a victory the nation is lost. Now admittedly, it is a bit of a stretch to assume that a nail missing from a horseshoe could have such far reaching effects. But the fact is that in the days of a blacksmith, the days when horses were the only means of transportation, it truly could.

And even if the blacksmith's creed is a bit of a stretch, it does speak to a truth, the truth being that we're woven together in such a way that what effects one person can and does effect another, that this world of ours is so closely knit, so closely connected, so linked together that some little thing can indeed have a profound and far reaching effect.

I do not know how many of you are familiar with quantum physics but, as I understand it, it's the blueprint scientists use when viewing this planet. It has come to replace the ideas and laws set by Isaac Newton centuries ago. According to quantum physics, the world is this sea of electrons and molecules and atoms and they are so delicately balanced that if a flock of butterflies moves a certain direction in the Far East it can effect the weather here in Buffalo. I know it sounds crazy, but according to several scientists, it happens to be true.

And while on the topic of electrons and molecules and atoms, I have read where each breath we take contains a few molecular particles of breath expelled just recently by one or another of the five billion people on this earth. We could well be breathing today what someone in China may well have breathed yesterday. And the particles of breath were breathed not just by people, but also by cows and horses and birds and bears. And according to Deepak Chopra, those very particles of breath have been around since the beginning of time and so it could well be that today we've breathed oxygen filled with the molecules once breathed by Jesus or Buddha or Confucius or Mohammed or one of the thousands of luminaries who have graced this earth.

And if you do not buy into any of the theories in regard to molecules and atoms and particles of breath, consider the disaster that followed the unveiling of an insecticide known as DDT, an insecticide which proved extremely effective in eliminating the insects that had historically ruined trees, crops, plants and vegetables all across our country. Upon its introduction, it began to be used quite extensively. Many a prop-plane was hired to spray DDT over various fields and forests while gardeners everywhere applied it liberally to their vegetables and their flowers. It wasn't until a few years later that several alarms began to be sounded as traces of DDT were found in the milk of breasts that fed hungry babies. It was surmised that the deadly ingredients of the DDT had entered into the digestive systems of animals and birds who had feasted on the bugs and fruits of those sprayed fields and gardens and, thanks to the food chain, traces of those very ingredients then made their way into the food of supermarkets and eventually into the bodies of mothers and finally into the breast milk the mothers were feeding to their children. What proved even more telling was that traces of DDT were found in the penguins of the North Pole so far did the food chain carry the deadly insecticide.

So even if one doesn't buy into the interconnectedness of the universe demonstrated by quantum physics, one can't argue with the interconnectedness of the universe demonstrated by the food chain. There's much to be said as to how closely knit this planet of ours happens to be. And what holds true for the planet around us holds true as well for the people around us.

I read something recently that I had never given thought to before. It's the fact that although there may be close to 200 languages and dialogues stretching across the globe, there is one language of which we all share. The cry of a child's pain is the same in Iceland as it is in India. The soft and wordless cooing of a mother as she lulls her baby to sleep is the same in Ireland as it is in Alaska. So too is the scream of a man in anguish, the sigh of regret, the sudden outburst of uncontrollable laughter or the piteous cry of a broken heart. Although we all speak different languages, there is one language common to us all. There is a string that connects us with every member of the human race.

And besides the common language, there are hopes, concerns and dreams which we all share in common. Back in 1978, the world community took the first tentative steps toward peace in the Middle East when President Jimmy Carter met with Anwar Sadat of Egypt and Menachim Began of Israel to negotiate what became the Camp David accord. The story goes that after a number of meetings, Sadat and Began could not come to any agreement and so they decided to return home. Began was packed and ready to fly to Tel Aviv, but before he went he stopped to say farewell to his American host. Carter thanked him and wished him well and then asked to see some photographs of his grandchildren of whom he had talked about earlier. Began took out photos and showed them not only to President Carter but to Anwar Sadat as well. Suddenly a flash of insight struck both Began and Sadat, bitter enemies for a long time. They both realized the string that connects them, their love and concern for their children and their grandchildren. They realized that when you scrape away the animosity and the culture and religious and ethnic differences that existed between them, one could see that at the core of their being rested the same hopes and concerns, fears and dreams. Upon the realization of that truth, they decided to sit down and work out a peace agreement and so they did. Besides our sharing a common language, we share with the human race common hopes and dreams and concerns.

And just consider how homes of today are touched by half the world. In the closet might be a shirt from Mexico and, under the bed, shoes from Taiwan. Hanging on a doorknob might be a jacket from Scotland. In the cupboards might be coffee from England and a flashlight from Hong Kong. The refrigerator might have beer from Germany or wine from France and in the garage might be a car from Japan. On and on I could go, but suffice it to say that besides the language, fears, hopes, concerns and dreams that we share with the rest of the world, we share each others goods, we rely on each others products, we depend on each other for most of our daily wares. We are interconnected not only with the world around us, but with the people around us as well.

And we can add to that the fact that we are interconnected with our God. There is this story of an Irish priest who hitched up his horse and buggy and went forth to visit members of his church. For the most part, he enjoyed the ride and the beauty of the countryside except for this one ugly field. It was deserted, abandoned, full of rocks and brambles with a broken down old fence. It was so ugly the priest could hardly stand the sight of it. Then one day a young man by the name of Michael moved into the area and bought that field. Little by little he cleared away the brambles and the rocks. He used the rocks to build a sturdy wall and he replaced the old broken fence with a brand new one. He planted a small garden and began to care for it. The parish priest, as you might imagine, was delighted to see how much the field changed and enjoyed viewing it as he made his weekly rounds. One day, as he was passing by, he stopped and went over to talk to the man who transformed the field. "Michael," he yelled, "may I have a word with you?" The young man stopped his work and came over to greet the priest. "Michael" the priest said, "I just wanted to tell you that this field is the light of my heart. You and the Lord are doing a fine job with it!"

"Thank you kindly Father!" the young man replied. "But you should have seen it when God had it all to himself!"

In everything that goes on in life, there is a linkage between God and us. There's a partnership, an interconnectedness between God and us. Just as that field was ugly when God had it all to himself, so could our lives and what we do with our lives be ugly when we carry them out apart from God. The beauty that emerges from human hands, the wonderful inventions created by human minds, the uplifting music emerging from human voices and the marvelous acts of compassion from human hearts all come to us compliments of God and we working as one. They are the elements of a divine thread running through this world in which we live and of which we are a part.

So when you come right down to it, the blacksmith's creed isn't really so far fetched after all. There are so many strings attached to us, we are so interconnected with all that is going on in this life and the life beyond this one, so interconnected with each other and the world that anything which happens to one single individual, anything which happens to any of God's living creatures does, indeed, register an impact. It does, indeed, register an effect in all four corners of the world.

I believe that to be one of the underlying messages of the Feast of Corpus Christi which we are celebrating today. It's a reminder to us all that we are members of the Body of Christ, interconnected with the Lord, divinely entwined with the whole human race. As such, every single one of us impacts the Body of Christ, every single one of us can and does effect more than just ourselves.

Betty Eadie who gave us the best seller *Embraced by the Light*[13] relates an incident that happened to her when she was just a little girl lying in a hospital bed. A nurse came into her room and when she opened her eyes the nurse said to one of the aides: "Such love and kindness come out of this little girl's eyes!" That comment so struck her, so affirmed her and so moved her that from that day forward she began thinking of herself as a kind and loving person. As a result, she has been spreading love and kindness throughout the world ever since.

That loving remark of that nurse plucked a string at Betty Eadie's heart some forty years ago and the reverberations from that pluck has spread to probably hundreds of thousands of people and is still spreading today. What it all means is that we must never forget that what we do matters, what we say matters, how we act matters. We are so intertwined with the human race, with the universe, with the world beyond this one that there is no way that we do not register an impact in the living of our life. According to the blacksmith's creed because of the lack of a nail the nation is lost. According to the creed of Corpus Christi, because of a lack of a kind word or deed on our part, a nation of souls could well be lost to love.

A Name and a Face

Scripture Lesson: 1 Corinthians 10: 16-17
"...We, though many, are one body..."

The feast of Corpus Christi calls us to view the entire human race as our next of kin.

One of the more fascinating stories from the First World War occurred on Christmas Eve of 1914. A quiet calm had settled over the Western Front as a battalion of opposing armies observed a 24-hour cease-fire. A welcome respite was thus provided for the English and German soldiers. It wasn't many hours into the silence of the night when one of the English soldiers heard what he believed to be a choir singing Christmas carols. All the Englishmen scrambled to the edge of their bunkers and sure enough they heard German voices singing "Silent Night" in German. When the singing stopped, the English soldiers raised their voices in song as they bellowed a version of "God Rest Ye Merry Gentlemen." Back and forth, both camps took turns singing Christmas carols. Before long, a German soldier waving a white flag approached the bunker of the Englishmen with a bag of candy bars. Slowly, men from both sides eased out into the neutral zone and in the moments that followed, something magical took place.

The soldiers began greeting each other and sharing gifts. They even shared the pictures they carried of their loved ones. No one knows whose idea it was to start a football game but with the help of flares the field was lit and the German and British soldiers played until they and the lights were exhausted. The next morning, they got together again and this time they played a game of soccer and kept up their exchange of food and fellowship. Needless to say, when the Christmas ceasefire came to an end, the war could not be resumed at that front. Both sides found that the enemy had a face and behind that face were human beings just like themselves and that fact made it impossible for them to take up arms against each other.

I was reading recently a piece by William March called Company K[14] and he told the story of the most accurate sharpshooter in the American Army in France. When he was called upon to exercise his skills and shoot at a particular member of the opposing army, he could not do it because when he got the individual in his scope and saw his face, he couldn't bring himself to fire his weapon. "It would be 'like killing a brother,'" so he said. This presented a dilemma to his commanding officer. How was he going to get the sharpshooter to do his job? He did so by switching the glass in the sharpshooter's telescopic lens so that, when he would zero in on a member of the opposing army, the soldier appeared so very far way that he no longer resembled a living person.

Terrorist and fascist regimes regularly put hoods over the heads of people they want killed because they have found that it's difficult for ordinary soldiers to shoot and kill someone who could look them in the eye. This all leads to the point of how attitudes change, beliefs change, thoughts and feelings change once we come to realize that the someone or somebody has a face, once we come to realize that the someone or somebody has needs and hurts and wants similar to our own. Down through the ages it's been shown time and again that the so-called enemy is not so easy to kill when you come to find that they're not the monsters they've been made out to be, when you come to find that they have flesh and blood just like you and just like me.

James Taylor wrote about that point in another way. In an essay entitled "The Family Way," he wrote as to how often we tend to be hardliners when it comes to crime. We believe strongly in the death penalty. We believe strongly in jail time without parole. All of that changes, however, says Taylor, once a family member commits a crime. We suddenly see things from another perspective. Suppose, he wrote, suppose that your sister committed the murder. Chances are we wouldn't be that quick in advocating for the death penalty. Suppose, Taylor wrote, suppose it was your son who got arrested for stealing. Chances are we would not be so vocal about jail time without parole. Our hardness, our absoluteness, our thirst for justice and vengeance gets tempered quite dramatically when the people deemed guilty are family, when those who did wrong happen to be our next of kin.

So not only do our attitudes, beliefs, thoughts and feelings change when that someone or somebody has a face, when they have needs and hurts and wants similar to our own; but our attitudes, beliefs, thoughts and feelings change even more when that someone or somebody happens to be family.

This truth applies not only to wars and crimes and wrongdoings but it applies to tragedies and disasters as well. Some years ago in a small village in the Midwest, a little 12-year-old girl named Terry was babysitting her younger brother. Terry walked outside to check the mail. As she turned back from the mailbox, she couldn't believe her eyes. The house was on fire. So quick did the fire take off that the entire house was engulfed in flames. Terry ran as quick as she could back into that burning house only to find her baby brother trapped by a beam which had fallen pinning him to the floor. Hurriedly, Terry worked to free her brother. She had trouble getting him loose as the flames were dancing around their heads. Finally, she freed him and out the door the two of them ran just as the roof of the house was about to collapse. By this time, the firemen were on the scene and neighbors had gathered and tended to her and her brother. They congratulated her for her courage and her bravery and one of them asked, "What were you thinking about when you ran into the burning house?" Terry had a great answer. She said, "I wasn't thinking about anything. I just heard my little brother crying."

It's amazing as to the lengths to which we'll go and the risks we'll take and the things we'll do when the someone or the somebody in trouble happens to be our brother or sister or our son or daughter, our father or mother. Surely we'd be concerned and upset quite naturally if anyone was in peril but the intensity level rises considerably as does our desire to help when the anyone is someone we love and care about. What Terry did for her brother would not be far from what we would do if our next of kin were in that burning house.

When it comes to the someone's and somebody's of the world, if you put a face and a name on them, if they're deemed as family, it makes a powerful difference. There's a lessening of animosity, a softening of hardness, a rise in concern and upset as well as a greater willingness to be of help. And it makes a powerful difference as well when it comes to appreciation and respect.

Upon graduation from college, a young lady landed her dream job. All her life, this lover of books looked forward to the day when she could read, examine, and catalog books on a regular basis. Several months into the job, she processed a new book and, upon examining the book, didn't think much of it. She deemed it boring and never bothered examining it any further. It just so happened that shortly thereafter she met a young man with whom she fell madly in love. On their first date, she mentioned that his name sounded familiar. Then, she remembered. "We have a book in our library written by someone with the same name." The man's face brightened as he replied, "That's no coincidence—I wrote that book!" When she arrived home that night, she couldn't wait to read it. She went to the library with her passkey and flashlight and, upon finding the book, discovered it was the one she deemed boring, the one she didn't think much of. She took it home and started reading it and she couldn't put it down. It was the most fascinating book she had ever read. "What," you might ask, "made the difference between that book being boring and that book being fascinating?" The answer is simple. She met the author.

It's amazing as to how our attitudes and feelings and thoughts and beliefs about a someone or a somebody change when we've gotten to know them, when we've gotten to learn their history, when we've gotten to learn about some of the particulars of their life. The experience of the librarian and that book is often our experience when it comes to that someone or that somebody we've gotten to know and meet. We appreciate them more. We respect them more. We think more of them because we saw beyond their cover and absorbed and digested the content of their life.

The essence of today's feast of Corpus Christi, what we actually celebrate on this day is that the someone's and somebody's of the world have a lot of content to their life. They are in fact sons and daughters of God. They are in fact our brothers and sisters. So they not only have a face and a name but they are members of our family. They are our next of kin. They are our flesh and blood. If we could but absorb and embrace that truth, the world would be a better place.

A puzzle page in a newspaper showed a drawing of an outdoor scene. Beneath it was the question: "Can you find the girl in the drawing?" A close examination of the drawing showed the girl's eyes and eyebrows concealed in a tree branch. Another branch hid her mouth and nose. A cloud revealed her flowing hair. Once you discover the girl, that drawing will never be the same again.

If we embrace the message of this Corpus Christi day and indeed see the somebody's or someone's of the world as fellow brothers and sisters in Christ; the drawing of the world will never be the same again. For one thing, we'll come to see the enemy, the murderer, the embezzler, and the crook as family and that should spur a softening of our hardness. For another, we'll come to see the man or woman in the burning house or in the soup kitchen line or in a broken-down alley as family and that should spur a greater intensity to help. We'll also come to see that inside the cover of each and every human being sits a child of God and that should spur greater respect and appreciation and love.

My friends embrace the message of this feast of Corpus Christi. Change your attitudes and beliefs and thoughts and feelings about the someone's and somebody's of the world. See God's eyes and eyebrows in them. See God's mouth and nose in them. See God's flowing hair in them. Do that and this world will never be the same again.

Secrets

Scripture Lesson: Mark 1: 40-41
"...See that you tell no one anything..."

There are many positives as well as negatives attached to secrets.

There was an old priest, who became very upset when people confessed to adultery. One day from the pulpit he announced: "If I hear one more person confess to adultery, I will quit this parish." Parishioners loved their priest and, not wishing him to leave, came up with a secret word for adultery. From that day forward, anyone committing that sin would confess that they had fallen. This kept the old priest happy and all went well. It went well until the day when death would claim that beloved priest. His replacement soon arrived and it wasn't long thereafter that he came knocking at the door of the local mayor. After the mayor's cordial greeting, the new priest proceeds to tell him that something needs to be done about the town's sidewalks, that vast numbers of people have been coming into his confessional talking about having fallen. The mayor begins to laugh as he realizes that no one informed the new priest about the secret word. Just as he was about to supply the information, the priest pointed an accusing finger at him and said, "I don't know what you are laughing about, your wife fell three times this past week."

I tell that humorous story because I would like to talk with you today about secrets. In particular, the existence of secrets, the keeping of secrets, and the telling of secrets. Secrets abound in this world in which we live and sometimes that is good and sometimes that is bad. Bear with me as I review the good and the bad of secrets.

First of all the secrets of the world have been the salvation of the world. I reference here the first four verses of a most familiar poem: "Twinkle, Twinkle little star how I wonder what you are, up above the world so high, like a diamond in the sky." The first inhabitants of this planet mouthed some form of that poem. Their thirst to know the secrets of the stars would eventually spawn the fields of astronomy and astrology. The impelling nature of secrets would usher forth the likes of Copernicus, Galileo, Kepler and Newton. And what held true for things above held true as well for things below. The desire to learn the secrets of the earth got people digging and that digging unearthed fossils and those fossils unearthed further secrets until the science of geology and paleontology were born. And why do you suppose we are spending so much time and resources today in the field of genetics except to say we are searching for the secret as to how this body of ours operates, a secret which we hope will yield the long sought cure for cancer.

So one could truthfully say that if it wasn't for secrets, there would not have been the growth and development of the field of science, a field which not only bred great scientists but also opened bodies of knowledge that have been crucial to the growth and development of this world in which we happen to dwell.

So, number one, secrets are great catalysts for the workings of the mind, great incentives for the advancement of knowledge and, second, secrets make kindnesses doubly dear. Two brothers, one a bachelor and the other married, owned a farm whose fertile soil yielded an abundance of grain. Half the grain went to one brother and half to the other. All went well but every now and then, the married man began to wake in the middle of the night thinking to himself: "This isn't fair! My brother isn't married, he's all alone, and he gets only half the produce of the farm. Here I am with a wife and five children. I have all the security I need for my old age. Who will care for my poor brother when he gets old?" With that, he gets out of bed, sneaks over

131

to his brother's barn, and then pours a sack-full of grain into his brother's grainery. He makes it a point to do that on a regular basis.

Ironically, his bachelor brother also begins to have trouble sleeping as he thinks to himself: "This isn't fair! My brother has a wife and five children and he gets only half the produce of the land. I have no one but myself to support, why should my brother, whose need is obviously greater than mine, receive exactly the same amount of grain as I?" So he gets out of his bed, sneaks over to his brother's barn and then pours a sack-full grain into his brother's grainery. He makes it a point to do that on a regular basis.

This went on secretly for years but then one fateful night it happened that they got out of bed at the same time. As they went over to their brother's barn, they bumped into each other, each with a sack of grain upon their back. When they realized what each had been doing secretly for such a long time, their love for each other grew more strongly and the story goes that when they passed away the town built a church at the very spot where the two brothers met in the middle of that fateful night. They could think of no place in the town more blessed or holy.

There is so much more to be said of kindnesses that are done in secret. There is so much more luster on the shine of a good deed done in secret and who would deny the truth that there's a higher level of character in those who choose anonymity over the accolades they'd surely receive from a deed deserving of praise. Jesus said as much when he told his disciples that, when they pray or fast or give alms, they were to do so in secret for it is only when they are not recognized publicly for what they've done that: "God who sees in secret will applaud and repay them."

Third on the list of positives involving secrets is the sense of trust and confidence and acceptance which they imply. I told my mother I would be preaching on secrets and she proceeded to tell me of a woman she visits in a nursing home who unveiled a deeply held secret that had been troubling her and bothering her for a long time. My mom said she felt deeply touched and honored that the woman thought enough of her and their relationship that she could safely reveal the secret which she held back from everyone else.

That is the beauty and the honor of being let in on a secret. It means people feel safe with you. It means people feel they can trust you. It means people feel you possess the inner discipline to keep in confidence what was given in confidence. That's why gossip is so vicious and so cruel for it means someone revealed a secret they had no business revealing, someone who had been given the privilege of confidential information defaulted on that privilege.

So when it comes to the existence, the keeping and the telling of secrets, there are many positives that need to be honored and respected and preserved. But along with the positives, there sits the negative. On February 9, 1996, a railroad train running from Warwick, New Jersey, to Hoboken ran past a red signal and smashed into the back of another train. The crash killed the engineers of both trains as well as one passenger. One hundred and fifty eight people were injured. One year later the National Transportation Safety Board announced the results of its investigation into the accident. The engineer of the train that ran the signal did so because he never saw it. For nine years, that engineer had been slowly losing his sight due to a diabetic condition and for all of those nine years, because he feared the loss of his job, he kept it a secret, as did his doctor. One could say in this particular case that the keeping of a secret had lethal implications.

A parallel can be found in such horrible crimes as domestic violence and physical and sexual abuse as well as pedophilia and incest. Be it fear or be it shame or be it terror or be it a perverted sense of social propriety, the families and individuals involved often keep those horrors a secret and because it is a secret, no action is taken to stop it. Even if help is provided in terms of physical healing, the psychological damage is massive and, from all accounts, the scarring it leaves behind often results in the victims becoming future predators. There are many things that shouldn't be kept a secret, that shouldn't be held in confidence, that must never be kept from the people in authority that need to know. So when it comes to the negatives of secrets, there is the damage, the hurt, the pain, the suffering it can cause not only for the parties involved but also for the generations still to come.

Then there's the heaviness and the pressure a secret places upon a soul. I call to your attention Karen Power. For 23 years she was a fugitive. She had driven the get-away car in a bank robbery which ended in the death of a policeman, Walter Schroeder. Able to avoid arrest, she moved on to a new city whereupon she established a new life. She took on a new identity, got married and had nine children and, from all accounts, was living a beautiful life. The problem, however, was that the secret of what she had done in her past was inflicting a heavy toll upon her psyche and finally, for the sake of a peace she couldn't feel, she revealed her secret to her family and then gave herself up to the FBI. Reporters wrote: "Serenity and relief and hope was etched upon Karen Power's face when the judge handed over her sentence of 8 to 10 years in prison." She was smiling the smile of someone who had been set free after years of unfathomable psychological torture, someone who had finally been unburdened of a secret that was destroying her soul.

Secrets often weigh heavy, especially when they involve a wrong that was committed or an evil that was done. That's why the Sacrament of Reconciliation is such a beautiful sacrament. Going to confession allows the individual to bare their soul, to unload their secrets and the lift which that provides can be unbelievably exhilarating and grace filled.

And finally, on the negative side of the secret ledger, comes the frustration a secret can provide. I'm reminded of a certain rabbi who had a weakness for golf. The only day he had time to play was on the Sabbath, a day when golf was strictly prohibited. Despite that injunction, the rabbi snuck away to a golf course where he would not be recognized. An angel happened to catch sight of him and informed God of the rabbi's sin. God told the angel that he would be sure to provide punishment. When the rabbi reached the eighth hole, God engineered a gust of wind which helped steer the rabbi's ball into the cup for a hole-in-one. The angel couldn't believe it. He turned to God and complained: "A hole-in-one? You call a hole-in-one punishment?"

"Well, think of it," said God, "who can he tell?"

There are many people deeply frustrated today because, for many years, they've kept secret their abilities and their dreams and their talents and their wishes. They've sadly done so because they feared embarrassment, they feared they'd be mocked if their secret were revealed. One can understand that rabbi not wishing to tell his secret, but it's hard to understand their not wishing to tell theirs, their not wishing to reveal their hidden talents and abilities and wishes and dreams. It is a shame how so many never reveal secrets about themselves of which they should be proud and not ashamed, secrets whose revelation could well have opened them to a richer and fuller and greater life.

Jesus in our Gospel today instructs the man he cured to keep the whole event a secret. He didn't want word of his miraculous powers to spread. Unfortunately, the man revealed the secret and Jesus was inundated with requests to heal.

I believe when it comes to secrets, Jesus knew of their positive and negative nature. He knew of how they could lure people to study and explore and investigate. He knew of how they would spark the opening of bodies of knowledge critical to life. He's recorded as saying how "the good deeds done in secret are better than good deeds done in public." And Jesus was also fully aware as to how being let in on a secret was a privilege and honor. And just as he was upset with the man who violated his secret, I am sure Jesus is upset as well when secrets hide information that should be revealed, when secrets needlessly weigh heavy upon someone's soul, when secrets frustrate the revelation of talents and abilities that should be made known.

My friends, consider the matter of secrets. Keep and nurture those that are positive, confess those that are negative and be sure that what's secret about you and your life, be sure that it can and will do you proud.

Flexibility

Scripture Lesson: Mark 2: 18-22
"...No one pours new wine into old wine skins..."

Rigidity can spell disaster in more ways than one.

A colleague once told of the damages he witnessed on the heels of a hurricane. He spoke of how the wind blew with such tremendous force that century-old trees, tall, hard and strong were felled, how everything sitting in that hurricane's path met with destruction and devastation that included homes, telephone poles and even sea walls. Everything, that is, except one group of trees. They're described as willow trees. What assured their survival was their flexibility, their capacity to bend and weave as the storm grew in intensity. They possessed an elasticity which allowed them to roll with the punches of the ferocious wind.

I'm reminded here of the Statue of Liberty. Designer Gustave Eiffel planned for its positioning just outside the harbor of New York City, a location accustomed to gale force winds. As a result, he provided the statue with a hollow iron frame which he then covered with a sheet of copper only about one-half inch thick. It was to assure that it could move and sway and bend with the winds. And experts will tell you it's the reason the Statue of Liberty's been so durable over all these years.

So whether it be the willows in the face of a hurricane or the Statue of Liberty in the face of the gusts and gales of the Atlantic Ocean, it could be said that flexibility is a key to endurance and survival. To be flexible is to be strong.

And we've seen that to be true not just with trees and statues, but with human beings as well. Psychologist Al Seeberg did a study of the personality of survivors of the most horrid of life's experiences. He studied survivors of prisoner of war camps, survivors of the Holocaust, survivors of the Russian Gulag, survivors of hostage situations and other varied imprisonments. What Seeberg discovered to be their most prominent characteristic was what he termed their "biphasic traits." They were a union of opposites when it came to their character. They were serious and playful, tough and gentle, logical and intuitive, hard working and lazy, shy and outgoing. In essence, they were extremely flexible, more so than most, and Seeberg tagged that flexibility as the key to their survival.

Think, if you will, of life in general. Those best able to handle its ups-and-downs, best able to handle the comedy and the tragedy inherent to life are those who can roll with the punches, those who, when adversity strikes, bounce back.

G. Campbell Morgan tells the story of a man whose shop burned to the ground in the great Chicago fire. He arrived at the ruins the next morning carrying a table and a sign. Setting up the table amidst the charred debris, he placed the sign upon it. The sign read: "Everything lost except wife, children and hope. Business will resume as usual tomorrow"!

So be it a gulag, be it a concentration camp, be it a loss of business or be it any adversity that can come life's way, those who stand strong; those who make the best survivors are the ones possessing the quality of the willows and the Statue of Liberty. They are flexible. They bend but don't break under the winds of pain and torment and loss.

And besides the strength and endurance and resiliency associated with flexibility, there's also the matter of the openness towards new thoughts and new ideas and new knowledge. A young man some time ago was holding in his arms the first very young baby that he had ever been allowed to touch. He was in a festive mood because the baby happened to be his very own son. As he was whirling the infant around the room, his wife kept cautioning him to look out for the baby's head. Checking the head, he was shocked to find a soft spot at its crown. In panic, he ran to his wife wondering if the baby needed medical care. "No! No!" she laughed, "Medical care isn't needed. Every baby has a soft spot on its head. It's there to allow room for the brain to grow."

So right from life's very beginning, there's been a correlation between flexibility and growth. One could say that the softness that concerned that father provides the wiggle room the brain needs for the reception and storage of all the knowledge and information that would be forthcoming as the baby moved on in years. So if we hope to grow and not remain stagnant; if we hope to expand on the possibilities for our life; if we hope to move into the future and not be mired in the past; we need "wiggle room," we need to be flexible, we need to be constantly able to absorb and receive new knowledge and new thoughts and new ideas.

Harry Emerson Fosdick once wrote of how in Neurenberg, Germany they once attempted to standardize music. A fellow by the name of Beckmesser came up with a set of rules and regulations which were to be strictly followed. In essence, from that time forward, no music was permissible outside of those rules and regulations. There was one way and one way only to write and compose and play music. No one argued with what Beckmesser had done. It was accepted by the people of Nuremberg as gospel truth.

Not long thereafter, a fellow by the name of Walter Van Soltzing came on the scene. Music to him needed to grow. It couldn't be held back by rules and regulations. So he composed and sang and played all sorts of music that didn't mesh at all with what Beckmesser held sacred. As Beckmesser was busy documenting all the rules and regulations that he had violated, all of Nuremberg was singing and humming and dancing to the music Van Soltzing had introduced to the German people.

Harry Emerson Fosdick referenced that incident as a lesson about the importance of flexibility. "You cannot bottle up what needs to expand," said Fosdick. "You cannot set in concrete what needs room to grow and develop. Those who are rigid in their thinking are destined to be like Beckmesser, moaning over the breaking of rules while everyone else is hailing and applauding the new, the fresh and the wonderful."

From 1900 to 1967, the Swiss were the world's leading watchmakers. In 1967, digital technology was patented and it was predicted that it would be the up and coming means for recording time. The Swiss rejected that prediction and stayed with the traditional ball bearing gears and mainsprings which had been the staple of watch technology for years. Unfortunately for them, the world was ready for that new technology and Seiko, a Japanese firm, picked up that digital patent and became the leading watch manufacturers in the world. It wouldn't be till they embraced that new technology that the Swiss would regain their former prominence.

Just as music needs room to breath and grow so does technology and so does medicine and so does doctrine and so does any set of rules and regulations. The universe is constantly changing and, unless we're flexible enough to accept change and to accept new knowledge and new thoughts and new ideas, our destiny will be similar to that of Beckmesser, similar to those old Swiss watchmakers. The world will pass us by.

So those who are flexible have great survival skills; they're strong amidst adversity; open to new thinking, and finally, they are able to accept and be tolerant of diversity.

I'm reminded of that wonderful movie *The Dead Poet's Society*, where Robin Williams played the role of an unconventional teacher. At one point on the silver screen, he encourages one of the students, Neil, to follow his passion, to pursue acting as a career. Neil's pursuit of his passion would never come to pass for his father forbade it. Neil is told by his dad that in no uncertain terms was acting an option. He's to go to Harvard to study medicine and that was the end of it. That father's refusal to even hear his son's wishes and concerns and objections would come to a tragic conclusion. Neil was found dead. He had taken his own life

It is a movie, I know, a fictional story, but it does capture the tragedy that can be had when there's a refusal to believe that there could be a point of view as relevant and as important as one's own. If a person we're close to and near is extremely rigid, it can well spell estrangement and separation and bitterness and rejection. Many a failed marriage, many a broken relationship with a spouse or child is all too often a result of rigidity, a result of a lack of tolerance, a result of not being flexible enough to observe and accept thinking other than one's own.

In our gospel today Jesus speaks of putting new wine into new wine skins. His reason for that necessity is the fermentation process. New wine will expand and bubble and contract for weeks on end and skins rendered rigid and hard by age could never absorb its changes. New skins are much more flexible and thus better able to handle a fermenting wine.

I believe Jesus used that imagery to stress the need for flexibility on the part of his followers. The new wine he would be presenting needed pliable recipients, recipients open and ready for change.

So our call is to dispense with our rigidity and to embrace flexibility. Our call is to be the new wine skins readily able to handle the new wine of the gospel of Jesus Christ. Answering that call will make us better survivors should the wind of adversity come our way. Answering that call will keep us from looking as silly as Beckmesser or as foolish as those Swiss watchmakers. Answering that call will make us more tolerant of varied points of view and thus less apt to be estranged from those with whom we differ.

I would like to close with something from a handout received at a conference:

"People are born soft and supple, dead they are stiff and hard.
Plants are born tender and compliant, dead they are brittle and dry.
Thus whoever is stiff and inflexible is a disciple of death,
Whoever is soft and yielding is a disciple of life.
The hard and the stiff will be broken.
The soft and the supple will prevail."

Elephants & Mice

Scripture Lesson: Luke 10: 38-42
"...Martha, Martha, you are anxious and concerned about many things..."

Trivial matters and concerns can breed tragic results.

One of my favorite stories involves a noted astronomer from the 17th century. His name was Sir Paul Neal and one day he triumphantly announced that he had discovered an elephant on the moon. His discovery became the talk of the town and not long thereafter Sir Paul Neal got word that the people were skeptical, that they didn't believe his discovery. The skepticism prompted him to invite anyone who wished to come to his observatory and see for themselves that there was indeed an elephant on the moon. A large group came and they took turns looking through Neal's telescope only to discover that what Paul Neal thought was an elephant was, in fact, a mouse and it wasn't on the moon at all. It happened to have gotten itself stuck in the lens of the telescope.

I tell you that story because all too often people have done as Sir Paul Neal had done. They mistook a mouse for an elephant. What they thought to be big and important was in fact not very big or important at all. And on more than a few occasions, it's resulted in many sad and terrible things coming to pass.

Of all the airline disasters this country has experienced, one of the most tragic was the crash of an Eastern Airlines jet into the Florida Everglades 10 or so years ago. The flight would become famously known as Flight 401. It was a flight from New York to Miami with a heavy load of holiday passengers. As the plane approached the Miami airport for its landing, the tiny bulb that indicates the deployment of the landing gear had failed to light. The question was: "Is the bulb burned out or did the landing gear not in fact deploy?" The plane flew in large concentric circles as the cockpit crew tried to determine the answer. Tragically, instead of checking whether the landing gear deployed, they concentrated on the bulb and got so involved in trying to remove and replace it that they failed to realize or notice that the aircraft was losing altitude. Soon thereafter, the plane crashed into the Everglades and scores of people were killed.

You could say that a tragedy unfolded because a mouse of a light bulb took on elephant-size proportions, because attention got centered on what was tiny to the detriment of what was huge. And so it's gone as well with other tragedies, some of a much larger scale than Flight 401

I don't know how many of the Irish are familiar with the battle of Drumcliffe but it proved to be a battle which should have never been fought. One of the combatants in that battle was St. Columba who was a monk in the monastery of Moville in Ireland. His adversary was Finnian who was the Abbott of that monastery at the time. The story goes that Finnian had just gotten back from Rome and now had in his possession a copy of the four Gospels. Columba asked Finnian if he could make a copy of that copy but Finnian refused. Not one to take "No!" for an answer, Columba decided he'd make a copy anyway, doing so piece by piece during the middle of the night while Finnian was asleep. Just as he was finishing writing his own copy of the last and final Gospel, Finnian happened to catch him in the act. That prompted a demand that Columba give up all that he had copied. Columba refused. Finnian went to the High King of Ireland to plead his case and the king ruled in Finnian's favor. Columba, however, refused to accept the ruling and the result was the start of a war culminating in the Battle of Drumcliffe. Thousands upon thousands were killed and all because of a manuscript.

The Battle of Drumcliffe, not unlike the crash of Flight 401, happened as a result of a mouse being made into an elephant, the result of a small problem getting treated as though it were of gargantuan proportions. And it makes you wonder about some of the other battles and tragedies that have plagued the human race and whether or not they, too, were bred in a similar fashion, whether they, too, came to pass as a result of trivial problems and frivolous concerns.

So our doing as Sir Paul Neal had done, our mistaking mice for elephants can result in the tragedy of lives being lost, it can result in the tragedy of people being needlessly killed. And it can also result in the tragedy of our fiddling with trivia while issues and problems of a far greater nature yearn for our attention.

When the Muslims were at the gates of Constantinople poised to take over the city, there was a church council in session not very far away and they were considering three questions. The first being the gender of the Holy Angels, the second being the color of the eyes of the Virgin Mary, and the third being the question: "If a fly fell into a vessel of Holy Water would the fly be sanctified or would the Holy Water be polluted?" This went on while the enemy was at the gate of the city poised for attack.

It is said that on the eve of the Bolshevik revolution, those "ten days that shook the world," a Congress of Russian priests met in Moscow for a two-day conference on the liturgy of the church. Six blocks from where the first shot of the revolution would be fired, the priests were in debate over whether a white surplice or a yellow surplice should be worn during a certain part of the liturgical season.

You might remember my telling you about a dorm meeting we had at the Seminary in East Aurora shortly after I arrived there for my third year of college. The whole meeting centered upon a rule stating that we could not drive beyond three miles of the seminary on any given evening. An hour was spent debating whether the mileage got clocked from the end of the driveway or from the middle of the parking lot. All this while race and campus riots were a regular part of the evening news and young men like ourselves were dying in Vietnam.

Unfortunately, all too often we treat mouse-sized issues as though they were of elephant-size proportions. We see a matter of negligible importance as though it were a matter of huge importance. And the tragedy comes from our doing so while there are matters of huge importance, while there are issues of elephant size proportions raging all around us.

And it can also result as well in the tragedy of a relationship, a friendship, a marriage coming to an end. If any of you are into theater, I would bet you've come to love and enjoy the works of Gilbert and Sullivan. I don't know if many of you know this or not but the two of them didn't talk to each other for years even when they were collaborating on a new musical and it was all over the matter of the color of a rug.

Some of you might remember my relating the story of a woman who was dying and how she severed her relationship with her only brother and it all had to do with an object from their mother's estate. The object was a berry spoon. She insisted it belonged to her while he insisted it belonged to him.

Time and again we've seen friendships die and marriages break apart and wonderful relationships come to an end, all because some mouse-sized issue became a matter of great importance, all because some minor disagreement managed to attain elephant-size proportions.

And then there's the matter of our peace of mind. Many times nervous systems have been shattered because a tiny worry or concern got magnified far beyond its allotted size.

I always liked that story of the man who went to a baseball game at Fenway Park in Boston. During the course of the game, a batter hit a foul ball that just happened to bounce in his direction and he caught it. He put it in his pocket and took it home. Instead of being elated and thrilled for having caught the ball, this man reacted differently. He took something that didn't belong to him and that bothered his conscience. So he writes a letter to the Boston Red Sox explaining his pangs of guilt and he enclosed a check to cover the cost of the baseball. The Boston Red Sox administration was very wise. They sent him back the check with a note that read: "Put your conscience to better use!"

I read of a similar story regarding a man who worked at a paper factory and inadvertently took home three sheets of paper and a small role of twine which he then used for his personal mail. Guilt got the best of him, so he goes to see his supervisor bewailing this terrible thing he had done. The supervisor couldn't believe the whining. He shouts at him saying: "How can you whine about something so minor as three sheets of paper and a ball of string when the world is awash, when your life is probably awash, with sins of a much broader and much deeper scale."

I'm not trying to minimize little sins, but far too many people utilize far too much emotional energy, they put far too much strain on their nervous systems all because of matters and actions and concerns hardly deserving of the attention they've been given, all because of matters and actions and concerns getting inflated to elephant size proportions while deserving mouse-sized status at best.

And finally there's the matter of our doing as Sir Paul Neal did when it comes to our careers. I happened upon a colleague who said that she had never met a retired person who stated that if they had to do it over again they would go to the office earlier or stay at the office later, that if they had to do it over again, they'd have climbed higher and faster on that road to success. On the other hand, she said, she's met numerous retired people who said that if they had to do it over again, they'd have spent more time with their family. They had come to see in their old age that it was their family that was the elephant and it was their career that was the mouse.

When Jesus admonished Martha in our Gospel for chastising Mary sitting in his company, he was telling her that she shouldn't have inflated the household chores to elephant size status, that sitting in his company was the far more important thing to do.

My friends do not make the same mistake as Martha; do not do as Sir Paul Neal had done. Too many people have died, too many people have looked silly, too many relationships have ended, too many nervous systems have been frayed, too many careers have failed to satisfy, all because little things took on a size and an importance they did not deserve, all because mice got mistaken for elephants.

Being Radiant

Scripture Lesson: Philippians 4: 4-7
...Rejoice in the Lord always!...

The ways and means of being radiant despite the problems and difficulties that come life's way.

In his anthology of the works of Rufus Jones[15], the great Quaker, Harry Emerson Fosdick reports of an encounter Rufus Jones had with Frederick Von Hugel who was, at the time, a brilliant philosopher. They were parting company when Von Hugel began talking about the canonization process of the Catholic Church. He began to recount some specific conditions which had to be met before sainthood could be bestowed. He spoke of how the man or woman needed to be loyal to the church. He spoke of how they needed to be heroic in word and in deed. He spoke, of course, of the miracles that had to be verified. And then he spoke as to how the man or the woman, through good times as well as bad, through prosperity as well as the loss of prosperity, through the mountaintop experiences of life as well as in the valley experiences of life; he spoke of how throughout all of those things, the man or the woman had to be radiant. Von Hugel then turned to Rufus Jones and said: "I am not so sure about those first three conditions for sainthood but I am quite sure about the fourth. If a person is going to be declared a saint, he or she must be radiant!"

I reference those remarks of Frederick Von Hugel because I'd like to talk with you today about being radiant. Not only do I concur with Von Hugel that saints need to be radiant but I also happen to believe that, if we truly are followers of Jesus, we should be radiant as well. We should be, as we heard St. Paul instruct the Philippians to be, we should be rejoicing. But the fact, however, is that we are not radiant and we're not rejoicing and we'll say: "How can we be so in light of the problems and difficulties that come life's way?" Well, first of all, it may well be that we need to focus our eyes in a more positive direction.

A farmer was working in his field when a stranger approached him. The traveler asked: "What kind of people live in the next town?" Without pausing from his work, the farmer asked: "What kind of people lived in the town you just left?"

"They were horrible," the traveler said. "They were dishonest, selfish, and inconsiderate." Looking up, the farmer shook his head and said: "I am sorry but that's probably the kind of people you'll find in the next town as well." The stranger moaned and walked away. Later in the same day, another man happened down the same road. When he saw the farmer, he called out: "What kind of people live in this next town?" Without pausing from his work, the farmer asked: "What kind of people lived in the town you just left?"

"They were wonderful," the traveler said. "They were thoughtful and friendly and kind." The farmer smiled and said: "I am pleased to say that's probably the kind of folks you'll find in the next town as well."

It just so happened that the farmer's granddaughter observed those two conversations. So she says: "Grandpa how come when the first man asked about the next town you said he could expect the people to be terrible. And when the second man asked about the next town, you said he could expect the people to be wonderful?" The farmer looked lovingly in his granddaughter's eyes and said: "My darling, no matter where you move or go to, you take with you your attitude and that's what will determine the makeup of the town."

The farmer was right on target. If we have our eyes honed only on the negative, if we only happen to notice the worst that somebody has to offer, then it's going to be very difficult for us be radiant. It's going to be very difficult for us to be rejoicing. With that kind of negative vision, every town we enter and every place we go, all we will notice is the bad and so we are bound to be miserable. To be radiant and to be rejoicing in light of the problems and difficulties that come life's way, we need to focus our minds and eyes and hearts in a more positive direction.

Second, we need to have hope. Victor Frankl, in his book *Man's Search for Meaning*[16], talks of the despair that overwhelmed him during his first days in a concentration camp. One day he looked out past the prison walls to the gray sky and the gray landscape when his eye caught a light that was turned on in a distant farmhouse and that light illumined the sky around the house. Something then stirred in Frankl's soul. He recalled the biblical phrase: "A light shone in darkness." He associated that farmhouse and its light with that biblical phrase. Suddenly his despair began to fade. Victor Frankl became a different person that day for he became a man of hope. He would spend his days thereafter stirring the embers of hope in those he came close to and near.

Hope can be a great elixir; it can keep someone radiant even in the face of the most horrible of life's conditions for it calls for their concentration on what can be rather than on what is. It gets them to see light where there appears to be only darkness.

The third way to be radiant and to be rejoicing in light of the problems and difficulties that come life's way is to involve one's self in a cause, to get into something that's bigger than one's self. When Havelock, the great English general, contemplated leading his men into battle, a battle he knew he'd be destined to lose, he never lost heart. He never lost his radiance. That was because he knew he was fighting for a just cause. He knew he was fighting for freedom. He knew that what he was doing was important. Musing over what was to come, he said: "If worst came to worst, we can but die with our swords in our hands."

I'm reminded of the artist living in a musty dirty attic, ill fed and ill clothed, yet beaming with radiance because he/she had a cause to live for, their art. I'm reminded of the research scientist who scorns the pleasures of life in favor of some library or some laboratory yet beams with radiance and they do so because he/she is lost in a cause, that of their research or their study.

I refer you to something the great Dr. Albert Schweitzer once said to a class of medical students who were about to graduate. He said: "I don't know what your destiny will be but there is one thing I do know. The only ones among you who will be really happy are those who have sought and found how to serve their fellow human beings."

Be it freedom, be it art, be it study, or be it research, or be it service to humanity. Radiance follows commitment to a cause for it gives one the sense that they are involved in something that is bigger than they are, involved in something that not only matters but matters a lot.

A fourth way to be radiant and to be rejoicing in light of the problems and difficulties that come life's way is to be someone of character. I like the story of the huge jet that was taking off one day on a particularly foggy morning. All the passengers appeared quite somber as the jet roared down the runway. The huge craft climbed into the densely clouded sky when all of a sudden it emerged above the clouds and huge rays of sunshine began filling the cabin. One of those somber passengers now had a smile on her face. She was heard to say: "I suppose every day is a sunny day if we could only get enough altitude."

I believe that is a good metaphor for life. If we are people of strong moral fiber, if we represent with our lives the best that can be found in a human being, people will look up to us. We'll have altitude and so we'll have the sunshine that accompanies it.

I'm reminded of the conversation Sir Walter Raleigh had with his executioner. The executioner told his noble victim that he would find the scaffold more comfortable if he turned his head the other way. Whereupon Sir Walter replied: "It matters not how the head lies so long as the heart is right." No matter how bad the circumstances can get in life, if we have altitude, if our heart is right, if we are someone of character, we can be radiant because we know that no one or no thing can take away our dignity, our esteem, or our pride.

The fifth way to be radiant and to be rejoicing in light of the problems and difficulties that come life's way is to establish relationships with magnanimous individuals. Many years ago a young man went out of the town of Devon, England to become a shipmate on the fleet of the famed ship captain Sir Francis Drake. Upon a visit back home, he met on the street an old schoolmate who appeared to be enjoying all the luxuries of life. He turned to the sailor and said with a smirk: "Well, it appears you haven't made much of your life."

"Well," said the sailor, "I guess I haven't. I've been cold, hungry, shipwrecked and haven't made a whole lot of money. But even though that's been the case, I wouldn't trade it for the world. Because," he beamed, "I've been with the greatest Captain who ever sailed the seven seas!"

Having friends of a great caliber, being associated with people of the credentials of a Sir. Francis Drake, sitting in the presence of men and women of extraordinary virtue and integrity; it provides us with a sense of honor; it instills us with pride knowing we've been privileged to have been included in their company.

And besides relationships with magnanimous people, one can also be radiant by establishing relationships with loving people. There is a wonderful story of a little child who accidentally broke a vase that was a cherished heirloom. The vase was a family treasure and the child, knowing so, cried out in dismay. Her mother came running and the child was shocked and surprised to see on her mother's face not anger but relief and concern. The mom gathered the little girl into her arms and cried out: "Thank God you are not hurt!" Looking back upon that incident, the little girl, now grown up, said with a huge smile: "I'll never forget how great I felt that day. I discovered that I was the family treasure!"

If we believe ourselves to be looked upon as a treasure; if we believe ourselves to be loved, if we know there are people who hold us dear; it brings a smile to our face and peace to our hearts and joy to our souls. It gives us cause to be radiant.

And then finally, the seventh way to be radiant and to be rejoicing in light of the problems and difficulties that come life's way is a recognition of and embracing of the things of infinite worth and value. I like the legend of the monk who found a precious stone, a precious jewel. A short time later, the monk met a traveler who said he was hungry. The stranger asked if the monk would share some of his provisions. Glad to be of help, the monk opened up his bag whereupon the traveler saw the precious stone. On impulse, he asked the monk if he could have it and without batting an eyelash, the monk gave him the stone. The traveler departed quickly, overjoyed with his new possession. A few days later, however, he came back. He returned the stone to the monk and said: "Please give me something more valuable and more precious than this stone! Please give me that which enabled you to so easily give it away!"

Having a large bank account and every jewel and every expensive toy imaginable and not a material worry in the world is not the impetus for a radiant life. That impetus comes from what can't be seen or bought or owned. It comes from the spiritual things that makes life whole and worth living.

So what Frederick Von Hugel singled out as the key element of sainthood is really the key element of a life of a follower of Jesus. For if that follower embraces the Gospel to its fullest, they will not only be radiant but they'll be able to do what St Paul instructed the Phillipians to do, they will be able to rejoice in the lord always.

That's because they'll have hope and they'll be positive and so they'll see light and good where others see only misery. They'll also be into causes bigger than they are and, even if the cause appears hopeless, they'll say with pride that at least they'll die with their swords in their hands. Having embraced the Gospel of the Lord, a follower of Jesus will always be at sunshine altitude for they'll be people of integrity and dignity and virtue and they'll be into the spiritual things of life so they'll naturally be linked with magnanimous people and loving people for that's what they'd be into as well.

With all of that going for them, with all of that being a reality, how can a follower of Jesus be anything but radiant. They'll have cause to rejoice in the Lord always in spite of the problems and difficulties that come life's way.

Giving Attention

Scripture Lesson: Mark 10: 46-52
"...Jesus stopped and said, 'Call him.'"

There's much to be gained from our taking notice of or our giving attention to those whom everyone else has passed on by.

A colleague paid a visit to his aunt who lives in a city some distance from here. Being the weekend, he looked for a church where he could attend Mass and his aunt suggested he go with her to the parish to which she belonged and so he did. When the Mass began, it was obvious that the celebrant wasn't much into liturgy. Singing was largely absent. The homily was abominable and it was all over in less than twenty minutes. My colleague was appalled. He questioned his aunt as to how she was able to stand such a terrible liturgy on a weekly basis. She said it was easy. It was easy because unlike him, she didn't pay attention.

It's paying attention that I'd like to talk with you about today. It's taking notice that I'd like to reflect upon with you today. And I'm not referring to liturgy but I'm referring to people who are hardly given any notice, people given little if any attention. Providing them that notice and attention can reap many a positive reward. First of all, it puts us in the company of some noble and distinguished individuals.

Several years ago a group of American theologians traveled to Africa to visit Albert Schweitzer at his jungle hospital. They spent three days with him and were greatly honored by the privilege of spending time with such a giant of a man. There was one experience during those three days that stood out from all the rest. They were walking together. It was close to noon and extremely hot. As they neared a steep hill, Dr. Schweitzer, who was 85 years of age at the time, suddenly broke away from them and made a beeline to the base of that hill where stood an African woman with a huge armload of wood. The American theologians watched with open mouths as Doctor Schweitzer grabbed some of the wood and helped that woman carry it up the hill.

It's interesting that Albert Schweitzer was the only one of the group who took notice of that woman. It's interesting that no one else's attention was drawn to that woman's distress except that of the 85-year-old doctor who would go down into history as one of the greatest humanitarians who ever lived. What often distinguishes the great from the not-so great, the noble from the not-so noble, is their ability to focus onto other people's pain, their ability to notice a tear or a grimace or a frown on the face of someone whom everyone else had passed on by. Time and again it's been shown that it takes someone of an extraordinary nature to look beyond their own needs and concerns and take notice of the needs and concerns of others.

So our paying attention to someone whom most everyone else has either overlooked or passed on by puts us in distinguished company, it puts us in the company of such greats as Albert Schweitzer, Mother Teresa, and Dr. Tom Dooley. And besides the company it puts us in, there's also the distinct possibility that our paying attention can provide us with the distinction of having made a difference in someone's life.

Desmond Tutu tells how in the days of apartheid in South Africa, if a black person met a white person on the sidewalk, the black person was expected to step off the pavement and into the sidewalk gutter so as to allow the white person to pass. One day, he was walking with his mother when a tall white man dressed in a black suit came toward them. Before they could step off the sidewalk into the gutter, as was expected, the white man did the stepping off instead and as they passed by he tipped his hat to the both of them. Desmond Tutu was shocked because his experience when it came to Caucasians was that of being ignored, overlooked and, at times, even beaten. Here was a white man giving himself and his mother respect and recognition. Inquiring about his identity, he came to find that he was an Anglican priest. Upon that discovery, Desmond Tutu was moved to consider a vocation to the priesthood, a vocation he would one day come to realize. One could say that a bit of attention spawned the career of one of the most influential churchmen of our time.

You'd be surprised as to the impact which the giving of a little attention can have on another person's life. You'd be surprised as to the difference we can make when we take the time to give a little notice to some individual everyone else happened to overlook or ignore. You can never tell as to the influence that notice or attention may provide. It may well do for some individual what that Anglican priest did for Desmond Tutu.

So our paying attention, our giving notice can put us in distinguished company; it can provide us with the distinction of having made a difference in someone's life; and it can also provide us with powers of healing.

The Bishop of Winchester tells the story of two officers who were lying badly wounded in a hospital. One said to the other that he really didn't care if he got better or not. The world, he felt, was hardly worth living in and for all intents and purposes he had nothing to live for. The other officer commiserated with him as to the sad state of the world but he did not share in the thought that life wasn't worth living. And the reason rested in a girl from Scotland who very much cared that he lives and not die. The Bishop of Winchester went on to say that, thanks to that girl in Scotland, the second officer stood a much better chance than the first when it came to his recovery.

I'm reminded here of Craig Shergold, a 16-year-old London lad, who got into the Guinness Book of World Records for receiving the greatest number of get well cards, 33 million in all, most coming on the heels of a diagnosis of a brain tumor which the doctors declared incurable. He is alive and well today some four years later. Although it may have been the radiation and the surgery that prolonged his life, there is no discounting the positive effect of having 33 million people tell him that they very much wanted him to live and not die.

One of the major problems of any illness is the isolation it instills, the sense that one's been removed from the mainstream of life. The lengthier the illness, the more grows the sense that life seems to be faring pretty well without them. The lengthier the illness, the more grows the sense that it really won't make much difference as to whether they live or die. Our giving them our attention, our providing them with the notion that we want them to live and not die could well turn the tide when it comes to their recovery. It could do for them what that girl in Scotland did for the second officer and what those 33 million cards did for Craig Shergold. There's no telling as to the healing our attention can provide to the life of some individual struck down by an illness or some individual wondering as to the sense of their carrying on with their life.

And that holds true as well for those who may not have any kind of illness or any kind of troubles apparent to the human eye. After Albert Einstein's wife died, his sister Maya moved in to assist him with the household chores. For 14 years, she cared for him, allowing his valuable research to continue. In 1950, she suffered a stroke and lapsed into a coma. From that time forward, Einstein spent two hours every afternoon reading aloud to her from the works of Plato. Although she gave no sign of understanding his words, he read anyway. If she understood anything from his gesture, she understood this: he, Einstein, believed that she was worth his time. That's the message we send when we give someone our attention, that's the message we send whenever we take notice of a particular individual. We're letting them know that they are worth our time.

Many a healthy looking child, many an illness-free wife, and many an apparently vigorous friend needs to know that they're worth our time. They need to know that they're important enough for us to take notice of them and their troubles and their needs. We may not associate healing with the healthy but the fact of the matter is that there are many healthy individuals whose egos can use some healing, whose esteem and sense of worth may not be in the healthiest of

RICHARD E. ZAJAC

conditions. Any attention we can possibly provide them, any notice we can possibly give them are sure to do a great deal of good for their hearts as well as their souls.

So our paying attention, our giving notice can put us in distinguished company; it can provide us with the distinction of having made a difference in someone's life; it can equip us with healing powers; and, finally, we may find Jesus on the receiving end of that notice or attention.

A friend was taking a tour of an inner-city church that was involved heavily in servicing the poor. They had this huge soup kitchen that was open to the public for lunch and dinner. He happened to come upon the soup kitchen just before the noon hour. There in the kitchen huddled together were the volunteers. They were about to say a prayer and so he huddled together with them to pray. Among the prayers lifted up, one that was prayed by an elderly African-American woman particularly moved him. She prayed: "Lord, we know you will be coming through the line today so help us to treat you well."

That African-American woman was on to one of the dividends that comes from the giving of our attention, from our taking notice of people, and that's the fact that Jesus may well have been on the receiving end of our attention and notice. And I am referring here most specifically to those who for the most part receive little if any intention, those who for the most part are given little if any notice. I'm talking about street people, alcoholics, addicts and misfits. I'm talking about those whose physical and mental condition makes it difficult to be near their side. They are those hungry and thirsty and imprisoned and naked people Jesus was referring to when he talked about the last judgment, when he talked about what he was going to look like when he will re-enter the human experience. So what you and I should be praying every day is a prayer similar to that of the elderly African-American lady. We should be praying: "Lord, we know you'll be on the streets today. So help us to treat you well by paying you a little notice and giving you some attention.

When Jesus in our Gospel today paid attention to and took notice of blind Bartimaeus, he did what no one else had done. He was taking

156

time with someone whom everyone including his own disciples had passed on by. In so doing, Jesus set an example; Jesus underlined the importance of paying attention to and taking notice of those who never seem to attract any notice, who are never paid much attention.

So, my friends do as did Jesus. It will put you in the company of such greats as Albert Schweitzer and Mother Teresa and Dr. Tom Dooley. You may make the kind of difference in a person's life as did that Anglican priest in the life of Desmond Tutu. You may inspire healing in a wounded body or soul. And you may, just may, meet Jesus along the way. So pay attention to and take notice of people especially those whom everyone else may overlook or ignore. It can and will pay many a dividend. It can and will reap many a positive reward.

Motors Always Running

Scripture Lesson: Acts 2:1-11
"...And they were all filled with the Holy Spirit..."

On Pentecost day, the Holy Spirit infused passion into the hearts
and lives of the Apostles

Not too many weeks ago, the National Football League held its
annual draft and each team drafted seven college players whom they
hope will make a significant difference on the football field when the
upcoming season begins. In the press conferences following the draft,
it was interesting to note a term that was used by general managers
from almost every team when they were asked why one particular
college player was chosen over another. That term was: "His motor
never stops running!"

That's what I'd like to talk with you about today. I'd like to talk with
you about the running of our motors. More specifically, I'd like to talk
with you about our passion, our zest, and our zeal. Time and again, it's
been shown that whenever it is in high evidence, when motors never
stop running, when lives are brimming with passion and enthusiasm
and zeal, much gets accomplished and more than a football team are
the beneficiaries of its presence.

Dr. Benjamin Bloom of the University of Chicago conducted a
five-year study of leading artists, athletes and scholars. He was
seeking to find clues as to how these high achievers reached their level

of success. He discovered in an overwhelming majority of the cases that it was their drive and passion, it was their zeal and determination, and not their talent, which accounted for their success.

Interestingly, a similar discovery was made in the world of business and industry and government. More than 58% of all CEOs of Fortune 500 companies had C or C minus grades in college. Nearly 75% of all U.S. presidents were in the bottom half of their school classes. And 50% of all millionaire entrepreneurs never finished college. What made it possible for these otherwise ordinary people to achieve monumental success was the fact of their passion, their zest and their enthusiasm. The fact that their motors never stopped running put them in a position to realize and achieve the success often denied to those far more gifted and talented than they.

And so it can be said for those who have achieved greatness. When he was a young boy, Michelangelo came to a master sculptor asking to be accepted as a student. As they talked about the commitment involved in becoming a great artist, the master sculptor said to the young Michelangelo: "This will take your life!" Michelangelo replied: "I know, but what else is life for!"

After a performance of one of his original compositions, a group of well-wishers gathered around Beethoven to shower him with praise. One woman remarked to Beethoven that she wished God had bestowed her with his genius. Beethoven replied: "It isn't genius, ma'am, you can be as good as I am. All you have to do is practice your piano eight hours a day for 40 years."

Georgia O'Keefe, the famous painter, was so committed to her art that she spent six months a year in the desert so she could better see colors.

Those who happen to wear the moniker "great" are usually those who locked into a particular vocation and never turned off their motor, never weakened in their resolve even though they were fully aware that their vocation would demand unbelievable sacrifice and unrelenting hours of practice and study and work. They had passion in their blood and enthusiasm and zeal in their soul and so the cost of their life's work didn't matter.

Then you have the matter of the inspiration. I'm not sure there's been a bigger inspirational figure in history then the person of Winston Churchill. And what made him such a source of inspiration was the fact his motor was always running, his life was brimming with passion and zeal and enthusiasm. It was evident in his speech, and it was evident in his spirit and his attitude.

Early on in the Second World War, things didn't look good for England. Nazi warplanes were dropping bombs and delivering unbelievable devastation to many parts of the country. Churchill went on the airwaves and delivered one of his most famous speeches. With practically the whole country listening to their radios, they heard Churchill say: "We shall fight in France! We shall fight on the seas and oceans! We shall defend our island whatever the cost! We shall fight on the landing ground! We shall fight in the fields! We shall fight in the streets! We shall fight in the hills! We shall never surrender!"

Those words resounded with such passion that it served to rally and inspire the people to the point where Nazi Germany stood no chance of handing England a defeat. People whose motors are always running, people who exude passion, are people who move us and inspire us and make us want to jump up to our feet to applaud and acclaim and follow them.

Who could ever forget that final scene of the movie *Rudy*? It was a movie based on the true story of Rudy Reutigger, who was not a very gifted athlete but managed to make the Notre Dame football team strictly on the basis of his enthusiasm and desire, strictly on the basis of the fact that his motor never stopped running. After serving on its practice squad for two years, he was finally allowed to suit up and stand on the sidelines for the final game of his college career. With seconds left on the clock and with fans and players alike shouting Rudy's name, he was put in for the final play whereupon he sacked the quarterback for a loss. The team responded by carrying him off the field, an honor that has not been afforded to any athlete since.

That's the kind of reaction that's often generated by those whose motors never stop running, those who exude passion and enthusiasm and zeal in what it is they're saying or doing. We can't help but feel goose bumps run down our spine and a part of us wants to put them on our shoulders and carry them off so others could benefit by their inspiration.

So, people of passion achieve the success often denied to those more gifted and talented than they, they are prone towards greatness, they are beacons of inspiration, and seldom if ever do they lack what they desire.

There's a story about Socrates that tells of a young man who approached him and asked: "How do I become as wise as you? How can I get the knowledge? Socrates walked with the young man to the beach and when they waded into the ocean, Socrates pushed him under the water and held him there with his hands. The young man pulled himself out of the water, gurgling for breath. Socrates pushed him under again. Again the young man surfaced and Socrates pushed him under a third time. Finally, when the young man's lungs were nearly bursting and he was on the verge of passing out, Socrates took him back to the shore and, with the man lying there on the beach gasping for air, Socrates stood over him and said: "Young man, when you want knowledge as much as you just wanted air, you'll get it!"

There's an old proverb that says, "When the student is ready, the teacher will appear." People with passion and exuberance usually get what they want because the intensity of their desire is such, their "ready" state is such, that it's unlikely to be denied, that it's unlikely that a teacher won't appear to give them what they want.

And right beside their receiving what they desire is their receiving a sense of contentment that will not weary or cease to delight. In his wonderful book the *Anatomy of an Illness*[17], Norman Cousins tells a story about Pablo Casals, one of the great musicians of the 20th century. Cousins describes meeting Casals shortly before the great cellist's 90th birthday. Cousins wrote of how it was almost painful to watch the old man as he began his day. His frailty and arthritis were such that he needed help in dressing. His emphysema was evident in his labored breathing. He walked with a shuffle. He was stooped over. His hands were swollen. His fingers clenched. He looked like a very old, very tired man.

Before eating breakfast, he would make his way to the bench of his piano, one of the many instruments he played. With incredible effort, he would bring his clenched swollen fingers to the keyboard. It was then that Norman Cousins watched a transformation. As he began to play a piece from Bach, Casals' old swollen fingers began to dance across the keyboard. As he launched into a Brahms's Concerto, his whole body began to come alive. By the time he walked from his piano, he appeared to be an entirely different man from the one who first sat down to play. He stood straight and tall and walked with vigor and vitality. What fed that transformation was Casal's passion; in his case, his passion for music.

When you have a passion for something, when something that's bigger than you are has your motor always running, there's little room for discontent because the trials and tribulations of life get trumped by what is serving as the source of the passion and excitement and exuberance.

Today is Pentecost Sunday, the day on which we celebrate the Holy Spirit revving up the motors of 12 listless dejected and forlorn individuals. A day on which we celebrate the Holy Spirit entering into the lives of 12 scared, frightened and lost individuals filling them with passion and zest and enthusiasm. Those 12 would leave that encounter totally changed and totally different and in a position to embrace many great and wonderful experiences.

Our goal today, our prayer today is that we leave ourselves open to the power of the Holy Spirit, that we too might get our motors revved up, that we too may get filled with passion and zest and enthusiasm, that there be something in our life, some cause, some vocation, some purpose to which we will direct boundless energy. We may find ourselves accomplishing what was denied to those more talented and gifted then we. We may find ourselves achieving the greatness of a Michelangelo or a Beethoven. We may find ourselves a Winston Churchill or a Rudy inspiring everyone around us. We may find ourselves realizing "what was wanted more than air." We may find ourselves a Pablo Casals quite content despite the trials and tribulations of life.

Gypsy Smith, the evangelist, told of a young minister who came to him asking for help in getting a church. Gypsy Smith asked him an embarrassing question. He asked him: "Can you preach?" The young man said with humility: "Yes, I can preach, but I don't believe I'd set the Thames River on fire."

"That may be so!" said Gypsy Smith, "But let me ask you this question: if I threw you in that river, would you make it fizz?"

When our life is over and God calls us home, God's not going to ask whether or not we set the world on fire. But he's going to ask if we made it fizz. He's going to ask if our motors were running when it came to matters and causes bigger than we are, matters and causes worthy of our time and effort. Unhappy will be God should we answer him: "No!"

Losing Jesus

Scripture Lesson: Luke 2: 41-52
"...Not finding him, they returned to Jerusalem in search of him..."

A look at the ways we can lose Jesus.

The day after Christmas, a priest discovered that the statue of the infant Jesus was missing from the Christmas crib. He looked around the church but it was nowhere to be found. So he sent word to the police and they began an all out search for the lost Jesus. Just then, the door of the church opens and in walks a little boy pulling behind him a red wagon. The boy walks directly to the stable and then pulls back an old blanket in the back of the wagon. Very tenderly, he lifts from there the statue of the baby Jesus and, walking over to the crib, gingerly and carefully places it where it once had been. The priest walks over to the boy and was about to reprimand him when the boy said: "Father, I hope you didn't mind. I came here last week and I told Jesus that I'd like a little red wagon for Christmas and I promised him that if I got one I'd come by and give him a ride. I came here a little while ago so I could deliver on my promise."

The story I just told is called the story of the missing Jesus and I tell it because I'd like to talk with you about a missing Jesus. I'd like to talk with you about a lost Jesus. With our Gospel today referencing just such a reality, I thought it would be good for us to consider how it is that Jesus gets lost in these days and times in which we live, how it is he comes up missing in more than a few of the lives of those claiming to be his followers.

Sometimes, Jesus gets lost as a result of a misunderstanding. I recently ministered to a woman who lost a child some 40 years ago and for some 40 years she felt that Jesus, for some awful reason, saw fit to take her baby away from her. The bitterness and anger that was evident in her telling me the story indicated that the years have done little to lessen her negative feelings towards The Lord. For that poor woman, Jesus was lost and missing from her life because she held him responsible for the tragic loss of her child.

I'm sorry to say that I've heard various versions of that same story all too many times during my ministry at Sisters Hospital and it's all the result of a misunderstanding as to the place of Jesus at a time of tragedy, a misunderstanding that finds him lost and missing in the lives of those who see him as responsible for something he didn't do.

And then there are those who have lost Jesus because he was misrepresented by someone claiming him as their own. A colleague, John Killinger, once told of a young woman who came to see him. She was intent on joining a church for she was attracted and enthused by what she had learned about Jesus on whose principles the church had been found. She had made inquiries of what it would take to be a church member and she learned the particulars. One day she happened to be driving by the church and, seeing a light on inside, she stopped. As she approached the door, she couldn't help but see two of the church's prominent members busy inside. She entered the church fully expecting to be given a warm greeting only to be met instead by a cold shoulder. That reception soured her enthusiasm for joining that church. She told Killinger that she no longer wished to be a follower of Jesus, having witnessed firsthand how badly they behave.

I'm aware of people who have had a bad and reprehensible experience with a priest or nun and because of that experience will never set foot inside a church again. For an unfortunate number of people, Jesus is lost and missing because someone who represented him, someone who claimed him as their own, behaved in such a nasty way or acted in such a horrible manner that they perished the thought of ever having Jesus be a part of their life.

And then you have those who once held Jesus near but then lost him amid the smoke of incense and the recitation of rituals and creeds. I'm reminded here of a shepherd's pipe that was supposed to have once belonged to Moses. Sometime after his death, it was decided that the pipe was altogether too plain and unattractive to have been owned by Moses and so it was embellished with gold. A few centuries later, some enthusiastic Jews decided to make it ever more attractive embellishing it further by overlaying it with jewels. Thus the pipe became extremely ornate but in the process it had lost its ability to play the pure and beautiful tones that were once its trademark.

I'm afraid that for many people the person of Jesus followed the fate of the shepherd's pipe of Moses. The person of Jesus got gussied up by artists and painters through the centuries. He's been cast in these glowing robes with a head of hair glistening as though prepared in an elegant salon and his hands and face looking nothing like the hands and face of a carpenter working in the arid winds of Nazareth. He's barely recognizable as a male let alone a human being of the first century. Add to that the theological treatises and pietistic devotions and liturgical rubrics that surround the mere mention of his name and you have a Jesus that can be likened to the shepherd's pipe of Moses. It's a Jesus who doesn't work for a good many people, a Jesus who is too otherworldly, too effeminate, too ornate, to be taken very seriously. You could say that for them Jesus is lost as well as missing.

And he's lost and missing as well for those who have embarked on a wrong path through life. Several years ago, there was a made-for-TV drama on the life of Marilyn Monroe. The movie started with her death where she is seen sprawled across her bed, her hand dangling over a telephone that had fallen to the floor. And there's a tape recorder present which had recorded the last hour of her life. A young reporter takes the tape from that recorder and plays it back and he's puzzled by what he hears. Towards the end of the tape, Marilyn Monroe cries out over and over again: "Tony, Tony, Tony where are you?" He does some research and as far as anyone knew, there wasn't any Tony on her list of friends and acquaintances. So the reporter began researching her background, looking everywhere for this Tony but to no avail. Finally he went back to the record shop where Marilyn Monroe had worked long before she became famous. He discovers that one of the clerks who had worked with Marilyn was still employed there. As the reporter interviewed that clerk asking all kinds of questions about the famous actress, he said something to which the clerk responded: "Oh, Tony would never have thought that way!" The young reporter was shocked to hear the name Tony so he says to the clerk: "I've been looking everywhere for this Tony. You're the first person to mention him. So tell me, who is Tony? Where can I find him?" The clerk replied, "I thought you knew. Tony was Marilyn's nickname for many years. We all called her Tony." Suddenly, it dawned on the reporter what Marilyn Monroe's cry for Tony was all about. It was a painful cry for the person she once had been.

Marilyn was a young woman who had ascended to the top of her profession in a flashy and sensational way. She had all that the world tells us we should aspire to and long for and want desperately: wealth, youth, beauty, fame, success, power, adulation. And yet somewhere along the way, she had lost Tony, she lost meaning in her life, and I might add she lost Jesus too.

Jesus talked often about the emptiness of wealth. He coined the famous phrase: "What does it profit a person to gain the whole world and to lose one's soul in the process." Had Marilyn not lost Jesus, had she not been far away from all he had to say about life, maybe she wouldn't have met her tragic fate. Maybe she wouldn't have lost herself. Maybe she would've seen that what she was gaining was coming at the loss of her soul. Many people have lost Jesus. Jesus is missing from their life because they walked a path that took them far away from him and his teachings. They embarked on a journey that would lead them astray from the values for which he had stood.

Then you have the matter of attention. Many people have lost Jesus though he stood not far from their sight. I don't know if many of you remember the story about a three foot statue of Cupid which had been carved by the great Michelangelo. It was missing for some

167

90 years only to be discovered sitting in a courtyard fountain of a hotel on 5th Avenue not very far from the Metropolitan Museum of Art. The irony was that hundreds of thousands of people had walked by it many a time and no one recognized it for the wonderful work of art that it was. It turned out that an art professor, who herself had walked by it for years, stops one day and gives it more than a passing glance. As she looks at it more closely, she comes to find that it's the treasure of Michelangelo that's been missing for many years.

Many people today claim they don't see or find Jesus anywhere. As far as they are concerned, he's lost and missing, some even going so far as to despair as to whether he even exists. And that's because they've looked for him in all the wrong places. They've not paid sufficient attention as to his whereabouts. Jesus, in chameleon fashion, often blends in with the environment. He often chooses to make appearances in the most unlikely of places. Like that statue of Cupid, many could well have passed him by never noticing his presence. They may have thought him lost and missing but he was there if only they had eyes to see.

And then finally, like Mary and Joseph, there are those who have lost Jesus because they've gotten too caught up in their daily chores. They've gotten too busy with life to notice that he's not in their company.

I like that story of a five-year-old whose parents presented him with a baby sister. As soon as she was born, he let it be known that he wanted to have some time alone with her. His parents thought this unusual, but he asked so often and so seriously that they allowed him to do what he wanted, to go into his baby sister's room alone. The parents stood outside the room as he went in and they listened through the crack in the door. The boy approached the crib and after a few moments of silence, he spoke to his baby sister. He said, "Sis, it's been some years since I was born. Tell me about God and Jesus. I'm beginning to forget."

Sometimes we get so caught up in our daily work, so busy with our lives, that we forget about Jesus. We forget the things he had to say. We forget to do what he expects us to do and it's not long before he's lost and missing from our life.

On this feast of the Holy Family, where our Gospel recalls to us the story of a lost Jesus, it gives us pause to consider the many for whom Jesus happens to be lost or missing. For those who lost him because they blame him for their tragedy, we ask for understanding. We ask that they may see him not as the cause of their pain but as an ally in their suffering. For those who lost him because they've been cruelly hurt by one of his representatives, we ask for healing. We ask that he may be seen in a person who is a genuine lover and follower of Jesus. For those who lost him because of incense and ritual and bad art, we ask for insight, the insight to see him as he really was and as he really is. For those like Marilyn Monroe who lost him on their way down a path that glitters with gold, we ask for help to save their souls. For those who lost him because they've looked in the wrong places, we ask that they have the eyes to see him in the many places where he makes his presence felt. For those who lost him because they got caught up in a busy life, we ask that they slow down and return him to their company.

Lord, Teach Us to Pray

Scripture Lesson: Luke 11: 1-13
"...Lord teach us to pray..."

A look into how prayer can be useful and effective and powerful.

I know that some of you have heard these before but please indulge me as I go over some old material. The first is a story of a young boy who wanted a bicycle and each night he knelt at the side of his bed and prayed: "Please God give me a bicycle!" This went on for an entire week and when the bicycle failed to materialize, the young boy took a statue of the Blessed Virgin Mary and wrapped it in a towel and placed it under his bed. That night he prayed: "Lord, if you ever want to see your mother again, you'd better get me that bicycle!"

Then there's the story of the three men in the boat, none of whom could swim. The boat springs a leak and begins to rapidly take in water. Two of the men turn to their leader and suggest he begin to pray. Joe, not a very religious man and a person not prone to weekly worship, folded his hands and prayed: "Dear God I haven't bothered you for a long time. If you would be so kind as to save us from drowning, I promise it will be a long time till I bother you again."

Then there's the true story of a rock singer who was asked about his feelings toward prayer. He answered by saying he was all for prayer. He was for anything that could get him through a night, be that prayer or tranquilizers or a bottle of Jack Daniel's.

The stories I've told are indicative of misuses, abuses, and misunderstandings regarding prayer. Although they may have been humorous, silly and far-fetched, they happen to be representative of how many people think and feel when it comes to prayer. Many have this idea that all you have to do is snap your fingers with a prayer and God will come running. Many resort to prayer only when the boat is sinking and the Jack Daniel's has run dry. And when God doesn't come running, when God doesn't provide the rescue or the tranquility, prayer is seen as a useless venture, a ritual lacking in effectiveness and power.

Well, I'm here today to refute that notion of prayer, I'm here to inform you that prayer is both effective and powerful. And if that has not been your experience of prayer, it could well be that you failed to take certain things into consideration. First of all it could well be that you did not fulfill your part of the prayer bargain.

I like that story of the team of Jewish boys who were playing their first basketball game of the season against a Catholic school in a Catholic arena. A few minutes into the game and a Catholic kid's at the free-throw line for a two shot foul. Just before he shoots, he makes the sign of the cross. The gesture baffles the members of the Jewish team and they look to their coach to explain the gesture. The coach replied: "It's called the sign of the cross but it doesn't mean a thing if he can't shoot free throws!"

Now one could well make the argument that answering a prayer concerning free throws would not be high on God's priority list, but let's suppose for a moment that it was. Why would God bother answering the prayer if that kid didn't practice free throws on a regular basis? Why would God bother answering the prayer if the kid lacked the talent it takes to play basketball?

I'm reminded of that apocryphal story of the man who prayed every night to win the lottery. Every night he gets on his hands and knees and prayed: "Lord please let me win the lottery! Lord please let me win the lottery!" And then, one night, he has a dream and God appeared to him and says: "Look friend, you've got to meet me halfway. At least buy a ticket."

One of the reasons why we may not have experienced prayer as useful and effective and powerful is that we didn't hold up our part of the prayer bargain, we didn't buy the ticket called work or the ticket called practice or the ticket called study or the ticket called dedication or exercise or diet or whatever.

Another reason might be that we weren't going to benefit by a positive response. One of the many stories involving the great Rabbi Abraham Herschel centered on a young student who came to him complaining of religious confusion and doubt regarding God's existence. The young man had been at peace with his faith. He had attended synagogue regularly. He read the scriptures daily. He had been a pious young man. But now, as a university student, he became beset with much doubt and he felt his faith slipping away. He shared with Rabbi Herschel his pain about those doubts and how the God of his youth had failed him. His question for the Rabbi was that if God indeed existed why hadn't he put his doubts and concerns to rest. Rabbi Herschel looked at him and said: "What makes you think God wanted your former peace but does not want your present pain?"

Now I don't believe that God gives us pain or causes bad things to happen to teach us a lesson or to make a point. That's something we might do and not something God would do. I do think, however, that some of the hard times of life can serve us well, that some of the hard times of life can issue in a wiser and sturdier faith, it can issue in the humility or the compassion that we may have been lacking prior to those hard times.

So it could well be that a particular cross we prayed to be removed may have struck God as one which it would serve us well to carry.

Yet another reason why we may not have experienced prayer as useful and effective and powerful is that we failed to check for residuals. Rabbi Kushner in his book, *When Bad Things Happen to Good People*[18], tells the story of a woman who came questioning the worth of the prayers said for her sick husband when he died right on schedule and died what could be termed a horrible death. And she wasn't just questioning the prayers of the rabbi but she was questioning as well the prayers of all her relatives and friends as well as the prayers of a prayer chain not to mention the prayers of two of the Catholic churches in the area. The rabbi gave a good answer. He said: "Remember when you first saw me, you said you were not going to be able to handle your husband's illness let alone his death and you, in fact, handled it well. Remember how you said you could never live without him and yet you are living well and you've been a source of strength and help to other widows." The rabbi went on to say that maybe the prayers didn't get her husband better but they did give her the strength to endure the tragedy and they did give her the ability to pick up the pieces of her life and start anew.

The great C. S. Lewis found the love of his life late in his life. He would marry Joy, which was her name, and a short time later, she developed cancer. His prayer, her prayer, the prayer of the congregation, the prayer of thousands who knew Lewis didn't appear to amount to anything, for Joy would die within the year. C. S. Lewis, as you would imagine, was beside himself in grief, beside himself in doubt, but as time went on, he slowly emerged from his grief with a faith renewed. His writing of that experience produced a book which became a classic. It's helped millions. It's entitled *A Grief Observed*[19].

All those prayers did nothing for Joy's cancer but they did help Lewis rise from the ashes of his grief and lead him not only to write a wonderful book but also to become a far more effective minister.

I'm a firm believer that there are certain things that God can do nothing about, that there are certain tragedies he can do nothing to stop. That being so, he answers a prayer by giving us strength and giving us courage and giving us friends and people to deliver the support we need to get by. C. S. Lewis and the widow referred to by Rabbi Kushner could have easily claimed that all the prayers said for their sick loved ones were useless and ineffective and powerless but there's the matter of residuals. There is the fact that they were useful and effective and powerful in the aftermath of their tragedy, useful and powerful and effective in a way other than what was originally hoped for, wished for or prayed for.

And then there's the matter of other forms and types and models of prayer. R. Maurice Boyd once talked to his pastor about prayer. The pastor said that most of the people in his parish say only the childhood prayers which they had learned while sitting upon their mother's knees. Boyd was surprised. Surely, he said to the pastor, surely they must have had matters of importance which needed to be vocalized by prayer. Surely they must have had hurts and needs which they wanted to bring to God's attention. The pastor told Boyd that the parishioners did indeed have hurts and needs and his parishioners did indeed experience consternation about a lot of important things but somehow, he said, somehow such deep matters never seemed to reach the level of a formal prayer. They were contained instead in the aches and sighs and groans and yearnings uttered before and after the reciting of those childhood prayers.

Reflecting on what was said, R Maurice Boyd posited the belief that God probably paid no attention to the childhood prayers of those parishioners but paid a lot of attention to those aches and groans and sighs and yearnings; that, in fact, the aches and groans and sighs and yearnings were their real prayers.

There was this scene from the television series *Nothing Sacred* that I shall never forget. It involved a woman who had suddenly become a recluse in her own home, a woman who had suddenly isolated herself from her husband and family, spending all her time in the dark. The nun in that series, the pastoral associate of the parish, was called to the house by the husband in the hopes that she might be of help. The nun immediately surmised as to what had happened and she coaxed the wife to come with her to church. Once there, she engaged her in conversation, slowly and gently moving it in the direction of the cause of the change in her behavior, the cause of the isolation from her husband and her family. It would prove to be the fact that she had been raped by a stranger while coming home one evening. She had kept that a secret and that meant bottling up all the emotions it brought forward and then hiding away in a darkened room. When the nun got her to talk about that secret, those pent-up emotions came roaring out and she let out a blood-curdling scream that rang through the empty church as though a cannon had been fired. The reason that nun brought that woman to church was that she believed prayer could initiate the healing process. Her prayer was that scream and that prayer did serve as a source of healing.

Now we never think of prayer as aches and groans and yearnings and screams but those are products of the depths of our being which is precisely the origin of a true utterance of prayer. Couple that with the fact that St. Paul tells us that God knows us best at the level of our groaning and you have a pretty good case for aches and screams and groans and yearnings as forms of prayer. So it could well be that the reason we have found prayer to be useless and ineffective and powerless is that we only looked at the prayers we utter in church or at our bedsides and we didn't look at all the other forms and models of prayer, we did not look at the countless ways we speak to God from the depths of our being, ways which have proven to be useful and powerful and effective.

Today's Gospel finds the disciples asking Jesus to teach them to pray and so he did and so they experienced the beauty and benefit of prayer. If Jesus was to teach us about prayer today, he might suggest we buy a lottery ticket before mouthing a prayer of petition. He'd probably tell us that sometimes it is in our own best interest that a prayer go unanswered. If Jesus were to teach us to pray, he'd probably tell us that God can't deliver on certain requests but there would always be residuals. He'd also teach us that there's more than one way to pray. My friends take those lessons to heart. If you do, you'll find that prayer is useful and powerful and effective.

Endnotes

[1] Ann Kaiser Stearns, *Living Through Personal Crisis* (Chicago: The Thomas More Press, 1984).

[2] Harold S. Kushner. *When Bad Things Happen to Good People* (New York: Schocken Books, 1981).

[3] Described by F.W. Boreham, *The Prodigal* (London: Epworth Press, 1941), p. 79.

[4] Dan Wakefield, *Creating from the Spirit* (New York: Ballantine Books, 1996).

[5] F.W. Boreham, *Mushrooms on the Moor* (New York: Abingdon Press, 1915), p. 257.

[6] Florence L. Barclay, *The Rosary* (New York: G.P. Putmans Sons, 1911).

[7] Wallace Stegner, *Second Growth* (Nebraska: University of Nebraska Press, 1988).

[8] 1 Harper Lee, *To Kill a Mockingbird* (New York: Warner Books, 1962).

[9] F.W. Boreham, *The Passing of John Broadbanks* (London: Epworth Press, 1936), p.159.

[10] AJ. Cronin, *The Citadel* (Boston: Little, Brown and Company, 1938).

[11] Ariel Dorfman, *Death and the Maiden* (New York: Penguin Press, 1992).

[12] Howard K. Smith, *Last Train from Berlin* (Phoenix: Phoenix Press, 2001).

[13] Betty J. Eadie, *Embraced by the Light* (New York: Bantam Books, 1994).

[14] Described by Halford E. Luccock, *Christianity and the Individual in a World of Crowds* (Nashville: Cokesbury Press, 1937) p.44.

[15] Harry Emerson Fosdick, *Rufus Jones Speaks to Our Time* (New York: The Macmillan Co. 1951) p.237.

[16] Victor E. Frankl, *Man's Search for Meaning* (New York: Schuster & Schuster, 1959).

[17] Norman Cousins, *The Anatomy of an Illness* (New York: Bantam Books, 1979).

[18] Kushner, *When Bad Things Happen to Good People*

[19] C. S. Lewis, *A Grief Observed* (New York: Bantam Books, 1976).

Also available from PublishAmerica

A DEER IN WINTER
by Michelle Ordynans

A Deer in Winter is an inspiring story of survival. It's the semi-autobiographical tale of a young woman's odyssey as she escapes from an abusive home, endures homelessness in the cold of a New York winter, and survives sexual attacks and harassment. In the meantime, she continues her last term of high school while secretly homeless, in constant fear of being discovered and returned to her abusive household. Through it all, she sets her sights on meeting her ultimate goal— graduating high school and attending college in the fall so that she can eventually rise above her troubled background and build a better life for herself. All the rituals of daily life must be negotiated: how and where she sleeps each night, in the rain and snow; how she gets food; how she cleans herself and her clothes; and how she spends her evenings. Along the way she works, makes friends and boyfriends, and explores the fascinating sites of New York City.

Paperback, 206 pages
6" x 9"
ISBN 1-4241-6999-2

About the author:

Michelle Ordynans was born and has lived in New York most of her life, with her early childhood in Florida and a few years in Israel. She is married and has two grown children and several pets. She works with her husband and son as an insurance broker in New York City.

Available to all bookstores nationwide.
www.publishamerica.com

TUNNEL OF DARKNESS
by Rose Falcone De Angelo

Why are some people given the ability to see into the future or communicate with the dead? Is this a gift or a curse? The visions come uninvited and change an ordinary world into one of marvel, turmoil and sometimes fear. This is the story of Bernadette, whose psychic powers begin at the age of ten and carry her into the strangest places.

Paperback, 241 pages
6" x 9"
ISBN 1-60474-153-8

About the author:

Rose Falcone De Angelo was born in New York City's east side to Italian immigrant parents. Rose moved to Florida in 1986. She is the author of a book of poetry, *Reality and Imagination*. At ninety-one, she is the oldest published poet in the state of Florida and has intrigued all who have the privilege of knowing her. She is currently working on her memoirs.